Test Bank

for

First Aid for Colleges and Universities

Test Bank

for

Hafen, Karren, and Frandsen

First Aid for Colleges and Universities

Seventh Edition

prepared by

Melinda Hafen

Allyn and Bacon
Boston London Toronto Sydney Tokyo Singapore

A Viacom Company
160 Gould Street
Needham Heights, Massachusetts 02494

Internet: www.abacon.com

ISBN 0-205-29579-7

Printed in the United States of America

10 9 8 7 6 5 4 3 2 1   03 02 01 00 99 98

TABLE OF CONTENTS

Test Bank

for

First Aid for Colleges and Universities

CHAPTER ONE
INTRODUCTION TO FIRST AID AND EMERGENCY CARE

MULTIPLE CHOICE

1.1 In an emergency situation, often victims who might have been saved die because

(A) those who arrive on the scene first are not sufficiently trained to give on-the-scene care
(B) too much time passes before proper emergency care is given
(C) emergency transportation is slow to arrive on the scene
(D) A and B

*Answer: D, Page: 2, Difficulty Level - M

1.2 How many Americans receive hospital emergency care each year?

(A) 10 million
(B) 30 million
(C) 50 million
(D) more than 70 million

*Answer: D, Page: 2, Difficulty Level - C

1.3 First aid is the ________ and immediate care given to a person who is injured or suddenly becomes ill.

(A) first
(B) temporary
(C) basic
(D) minimal

*Answer: B, Page: 3, Difficulty Level - E

1.4 One of the primary principles of first aid is to obtain:

(A) medical assistance
(B) patient consent
(C) emergency transportation

*Answer: A, Page: 3, Difficulty Level - M

1.5 First aiders can initiate many lifesaving procedures which include:

(A) airway and respiratory support
(B) bleeding control
(C) stabilization of spinal injuries
(D) all of the above

*Answer: D, Page: 2, Difficulty level - M

1.6 First aiders will always need a plan of action. Which of the following steps would not be included as part of a <u>basic</u> plan of action?

(A) observe the accident scene as you approach it
(B) try to make the victim comfortable and calm
(C) provide basic life support to those who are threatened; always giving first aid to the most seriously injured victims first
(D) have others direct traffic and position safety flares if necessary.

*Answer: B, Page: 4, Difficulty level - C

1.7 One of the principle aims of first aid is to minimize:

(A) further injury and complications
(B) pain
(C) the need for any additional care
(D) confusion and fear of bystanders

*Answer: A, Page: 3, Difficulty level - M

1.8 If you are alone and come upon an unconscious infant or child, you should first:

(A) activate the EMS system
(B) locate the parent or guardian
(C) provide one minute of rescue support
(D) provide three minutes of rescue support

*Answer: C, Page: 4, Difficulty level - M

1.9 In which of the following situations should a first aider summon more advanced medical help?

(A) childbirth is eminent
(B) a victim has been drowned
(C) a victim has more than one seizure
(D) all of the above

*Answer: D, Page: 4, Difficulty level - E

1.10 "Duty to act" means you have a ________ to give aid.

(A) choice
(B) responsibility
(C) legal obligation

*Answer: C, Page: 5, Difficulty level - E

1.11 You should provide basic life support first to:

(A) victims of cardiac arrest
(B) victims who are bleeding
(C) the most seriously injured
(D) victims in shock

*Answer: C, Page: 4, Difficulty level - M

1.12 The "reasonable-man test" is:

(A) given to first aiders to test their skills
(B) used to determine if the first aider followed proper procedures
(C) used to determine whether the first aider acted as a normal, prudent person would have acted with similar training, under similar circumstances
(D) used to determine if the first aider had good reason to implement first aid procedures

*Answer: C, Page: 6, Difficulty level - M

1.13 In administering care, first aiders are:

(A) bound by the same legal statues as other emergency care providers
(B) bound by different legal statutes than other professional emergency care providers
(C) are not bound legally

*Answer: A, Page: 5, Difficulty level - M

1.14 If the first aider acts with carelessness, inattention, disregard or oversight, he/she could be found guilty of:

(A) recklessness
(B) irresponsible behavior
(C) negligence
(D) intentional injury

*Answer: C, Page: 6, Difficulty level - E

1.15 In a true emergency with significant risk of death, disability or deterioration, the law assumes the victim would give consent if able. This kind of consent is known as:

(A) actual consent
(B) implied consent
(C) assumed consent
(D) forced consent

*Answer: B, Page: 6, Difficulty level - M

1.16 If an adult victim or guardian refuses consent, you may:

(A) not give emergency care
(B) give emergency care if you really believe it is needed
(C) summon the police if you believe that a life is at stake
(D) A and C

*Answer: D, Page: 6, Difficulty level - M

1.17 A victim should be considered infectious if the victim has:

(A) an open sore
(B) coughing or sneezing
(C) yellowish skin or eyes
(D) any of the above

*Answer: D, Page 6, Difficulty level - E

1.18 Infectious disease is a disease that:

(A) always causes permanent disability or death
(B) cannot be prevented
(C) can be spread from one person to another
(D) is untreatable

*Answer: C, Page: 7, Difficulty level - E

1.19 An infectious disease of particular concern to first aiders and others in emergency settings is Meningitis, which is commonly spread through:

(A) infected water, food, air, or direct contact
(B) sexual activity
(C) infected blood
(D) needles

*Answer: A, Page: 8, Difficulty level - M

1.20 To help you avoid being infected by contact with blood, body fluids, and secretions, you should:

(A) make sure your immunizations are up to date
(B) wash your hands after care with soap and hot water
(C) avoid touching your mouth, nose, or eyes
(D) all of the above

*Answer: D, Page: 8-9, Difficulty level E

TRUE / FALSE

1.21 Properly trained first aiders can replace the physician, nurse, or paramedic:

*Answer: False, Page: 3, Difficulty level - E

1.22 When a person is injured, a first aider should take charge and administer first aid while arranging for medical assistance.

*Answer: True, Page: 3, Difficulty level - M

1.23 Good Samaritan laws are enacted to protect the first aider from being sued unless the first aider is found guilty of negligence.

*Answer: True, Page: 6, Difficulty level - M

1.24 A competent adult has the right to refuse emergency care for himself/herself or a minor in need of such care.

*Answer: True, Page: 6, Difficulty level - M

1.25 If you wear latex gloves while treating a victim, it isn't necessary to wash your hands after.

*Answer: False, Page: 7, Difficulty level - E

1.26 You can be legally charged with battery if you give emergency care or forcibly transport a victim who has refused consent.

*Answer: True, Page: 6, Difficulty Level - M

1.27 There is currently no effective treatment for or vaccine against Hepatitis C.

*Answer: True, Page: 8, Difficulty Level - M

CHAPTER TWO
ANATOMY AND PHYSIOLOGY OF BODY SYSTEMS

MULTIPLE CHOICE

2.1 If the victim is standing erect, arms down to the sides and the palms facing you, what position is he or she in?

(A) lateral recumbent
(B) prone
(C) supine
(D) anatomical

*Answer: (D), Page: 17, Difficulty Level - M

2.2 A victim lying on his or her back is in what position?

(A) supine
(B) prone
(C) lateral recumbent
(D) anatomical

*Answer: (A), Page: 17, Difficulty Level - M

2.3 The victim is lying face down. What position is he or she in?

(A) anatomical
(B) supine
(C) prone
(D) lateral recumbent

*Answer: (C), Page: 17, Difficulty Level - M

2.4 If the victim is lying on the left or right side, what position is he or she in?

(A) supine
(B) prone
(C) anatomical
(D) lateral recumbent

*Answer: D, Page: 17, Difficulty Level - M

2.5 The term of direction that indicates toward the head is:

(A) superior
(B) inferior
(C) anterior
(D) posterior

*Answer: A, Page: 17, Difficulty Level - M

2.6 The term of direction and location that means toward the front is:

(A) posterior
(B) anterior
(C) superior
(D) inferior

*Answer: B, Page: 18, Difficulty Level - M

2.7 The term proximal means:

(A) to the left or right of the midline
(B) near the point you are referring to
(C) far away from the point you are referring to
(D) near the surface

*Answer: B, Page: 18, Difficulty Level - M

2.8 The term medial means:

(A) to the left or right of the midline
(B) remote from the surface
(C) toward the midline or center of the body
(D) near the surface

*Answer: C, Page: 18, Difficulty Level - M

2.9 The term of direction and location that means near the surface is:

(A) internal
(B) external
(C) deep
(D) superficial

*Answer: D, Page: 18, Difficulty Level - M

2.10 The function of the ligaments is to connect:

(A) bone to bone
(B) bone to muscle
(C) muscle to muscle

*Answer: A, Page: 18, Difficulty Level - M

2.11 How many bones make up the adult skeleton?

(A) 106
(B) 226
(C) 206
(D) 156

*Answer: C, Page: 19, Difficulty Level - E

2.12 The elbow and knee are examples of what type of joint?

(A) ball-and-socket
(B) hinge
(C) pivot
(D) gliding

*Answer: B, Page: 21, Difficulty Level - M

2.13 An example of a gliding joint would be:

(A) the shoulder
(B) the neck
(C) the ankle
(D) the hand

*Answer: D, Page: 21, Difficulty Level - M

2.14 An example of a ball-and-socket joint would be:

(A) the shoulder
(B) the neck
(C) the ankle
(D) the hand

*Answer: A, Page: 21, Difficulty Level - M

2.15 A modified ball-and-socket joint such as the wrist would be a:

(A) condyloid joint
(B) saddle joint
(C) gliding joint
(D) hinge joint

*Answer: A, Page: 21, Difficulty Level - M

2.16 The muscle that over which there is little or no conscious control is a:

(A) cardiac muscle
(B) smooth muscle
(C) voluntary muscle
(D) skeletal muscle

*Answer: B, Page: 22, Difficulty Level - M

2.17 Muscles that make walking, smiling, talking and swallowing possible are:

(A) voluntary muscles
(B) involuntary muscles
(C) smooth muscles
(D) cardiac muscles

*Answer: A, Page: 22, Difficulty Level - M

2.18 Oxygenated blood is carried form the heart to the cells of the body by the:

(A) capillaries
(B) venules
(C) veins
(D) arteries

*Answer: D, Page: 23, Difficulty Level - M

2.19 The function of the veins is to:

(A) exchange fluid, oxygen and carbon dioxide between the blood and tissue cells
(B) carry oxygenated blood from the heart to the cells of the body
(C) carry oxygen-poor blood back to the heart

*Answer: C, Page: 23, Difficulty Level - M

2.20 The passage of air into and out of the lungs is called:

(A) respiration
(B) inhalation
(C) inspiration
(D) exhalation

*Answer: A, Page: 27, Difficulty Level - M

2.21 A function of the digestive system is to:

(A) ingest and carry food
(B) absorb nutrients
(C) eliminate wastes
(D) all of the above are functions of the digestive system

*Answer: D, Page: 27, Difficulty Level - M

2.22 Which of the following is <u>not</u> a function of the urinary system?

(A) help maintain the delicate balance of water and other chemicals needed for survival
(B) return useful products to the bladder
(C) absorb important nutrients
(D) remove and eliminate wastes from the blood stream

*Answer: C, Page: 28, Difficulty Level - M

2.23 Endocrine glands secrete __________ directly into the bloodstream.

(A) wastes
(B) hormones
(C) chemicals
(D) fluids

*Answer: B, Page: 28, Difficulty Level - M

2.24 The two main structural divisions of the nervous system are the:

(A) voluntary and autonomic nervous systems
(B) sympathetic and parasympathetic nervous systems
(C) central and peripheral nervous systems
(D) none of the above

*Answer: C, Page: 29, Difficulty Level - M

2.25 There are two functional divisions of the nervous system. They are the __________ nervous system and the __________ nervous system.

(A) voluntary, autonomic
(B) sympathetic, parasympathetic
(C) central, peripheral
(D) none of the above

*Answer: A, Page: 29, Difficulty Level - M

2.26 The part of the nervous system that responds to stress with the classic fight or flight syndrome is the:

(A) parasympathetic
(B) sympathetic
(C) voluntary
(D) peripheral

*Answer: B, Page: 29, Difficulty Level - M

2.27 The nervous system has two main functions; communication and ___________.

(A) sensation
(B) reaction
(C) control
(D) none of the above

*Answer: C, Page: 29, Difficulty Level - M

2.28 The part of the nervous system that influences the activities of the involuntary muscles and glands is the:

(A) peripheral
(B) involuntary
(C) parasympathetic
(D) autonomic

*Answer: D, Page: 29, Difficulty Level - M

2.29 Which one of the following is not contained in the dermis layer of skin?

(A) sweat glands
(B) sensory nerves
(C) hair follicles
(D) cells that give the skin its color

*Answer: D, Page: 31, Difficulty Level - M

2.30 The subcutaneous tissue serves to:

(A) give pigment to the skin
(B) house blood vessels
(C) insulate the body
(D) none of the above

*Answer: C, Page: 32, Difficulty Level - M

2.31 The normal breathing rate at rest for adults is:

(A) 25-50
(B) 15-30
(C) 12-20
(D) none of the above

*Answer: C, Page: 27, Difficulty Level – M

TRUE / FALSE

2.32 Anatomy deals with the functions of the living body and its parts.

*Answer: True, Page: 16, Difficulty Level - M

2.33 The victim is lying face down on his stomach. The victim is in supine position.

*Answer: False, Page: 17, Difficulty Level - M

2.34 Bones and their adjacent tissues help to move, support, and protect the vital organs.

*Answer: True, Page: 18, Difficulty Level E

2.35 The structure of the joint determines the kind of movement that is possible because the bone ends articulate at the joint.

*Answer: True, Page: 19, Difficulty Level - M

2.36 Smooth muscle is also known as voluntary muscle.

*Answer: False, Page: 22, Difficulty Level - E

2.37 Cardiac muscle is able to stimulate itself into contraction without signals from the central nervous system.

*Answer: True, Page:23, Difficulty Level – C

2.38 The circulatory system has two major fluid transportation systems: the cardiovascular and the lymphatic.

*Answer: True, Page: 23, Difficulty Level - M

2.39 Digestion consists of two processes: the mechanical process and the chemical process.

*Answer: True, Page: 27, Difficulty Level - M

2.40 The elimination of digestive wastes is called peristalsis.

*Answer: False, Page: 27, Difficulty Level - M

2.41 The parasympathetic nervous system regulates heart action and supplies blood to the arteries.

*Answer: False, Page: 29, Difficulty Level - M

2.42 Emergency care is required for any blunt or penetrating injury to the abdomen.

*Answer: True, Page: 28, Difficulty Level - E

CHAPTER THREE
VICTIM ASSESSMENT

MULTIPLE CHOICE

3.1 Which of the following steps of victim assessment would you generally do first after arriving at the scene of an accident?

(A) determine the chief complaint
(B) establish rapport and control
(C) assess vital signs
(D) take a history

*Answer: B, Page: 39, Difficulty Level - M

3.2 To establish rapport with the victim and gain control of the situation, you need to use the three C's. Which one of the following is <u>not</u> one of the "three C's"?

(A) control
(B) confidence
(C) competence
(D) compassion

*Answer: A, Page: 39, Difficulty Level - M

3.3 Throughout the assessment and treatment process, keep your eye level __________ that of the victim.

(A) above
(B) even with
(C) below

*Answer: A, Page: 39, Difficulty Level - E

3.4 The major goal of the primary survey is to:

(A) get the person's medical history
(B) get the person's consent to treat
(C) check for life-threatening problems
(D) identify any witnesses

*Answer: C, Page: 40, Difficulty Level - M

3.5 Unless you find a life-threatening situation that requires immediate treatment, the primary survey should take:

(A) not more than 10 minutes
(B) 5 - 10 minutes
(C) 3 - 5 minutes
(D) one minute or less

*Answer: D, Page: 40, Difficulty Level - M

3.6 The final step in the primary survey is to determine:

(A) nervous system disability
(B) life-threatening problems
(C) whether blood is circulating properly
(D) if the victim is breathing and has a pulse

*Answer: A, Page: 43, Difficulty Level - M

3.7 The look-listen-feel technique is used to determine:

(A) whether the airway is open
(B) adequate blood circulation
(C) adequate breathing
(D) cervical spine deformity

*Answer: C, Page: 41, Difficulty Level - M

3.8 If the patient is pulseless, breathless, and unresponsive, begin cardiopulmonary resuscitation and continue:

(A) for five minutes
(B) until circulation resumes
(C) you are relieved by trained emergency personnel
(D) B or C

*Answer: D, Page: 42, Difficulty Level - M

3.9 The only kind of bleeding that should be treated during the primary survey is:

(A) bleeding from the chest
(B) bleeding from the head
(C) hemorrhage
(D) all of the above should be treated during the primary survey

*Answer: C, Page: 42, Difficulty Level - M

3.10 If you suspect a neck or spinal injury, you should:

(A) immobilize the neck
(B) activate the EMS system
(C) tell the victim to lie very still
(D) all of the above

*Answer: D, Page: 44, Difficulty Level - M

3.11 A neuro exam checks all of the following <u>except:</u>

(A) psychological functions
(B) motor functions
(C) sensory functions
(D) level of consciousness

*Answer: A, Page: 43, Difficulty Level - C

3.12 During the primary survey, assess vital signs using:

(A) technical equipment
(B) your senses
(C) your intuition
(D) a second opinion

*Answer: B, Page: 44, Difficulty Level - M

3.13 The answer to the questions "tell me where you hurt" is:

(A) a sign of the injury
(B) a symptom of the patient's condition
(C) the chief complaint
(D) the patient's assessment of his or her condition

*Answer: C, Page: 44, Difficulty Level - M

3.14 Vital signs should be taken repeatedly at:

(A) one to three minute intervals
(B) two to five minute intervals
(C) five to seven minute intervals
(D) one to five minute intervals

*Answer: B, Page: 44, Difficulty Level - M

3.15 The average normal rate of respiration for an adult is:

(A) twelve to twenty times per minute
(B) fifteen to twenty-five times per minute
(C) twenty to thirty times per minute
(D) none of the above

*Answer: A, Page: 45, Difficulty Level - M

3.16 Skin color can tell you a lot about a victim. If the skin is bluish in color it is most likely an indication of:

(A) high blood pressure
(B) shock
(C) lack of oxygen
(D) alcohol abuse

*Answer: C, Page: 46, Difficulty Level - M

3.17 Capillary refill is one method of checking for:

(A) fever
(B) high blood pressure
(C) carbon monoxide poisoning
(D) shock

*Answer: D, Page: 46, Difficulty Level - C

3.18 The best place to take the pulse of a conscious victim is at the:

(A) back of the neck
(B) wrist
(C) chest
(D) carotid artery

*Answer: B, Page: 45, Difficulty Level - M

3.19 An abnormally high temperature might be an indication of:

(A) shock
(B) spinal injury
(C) heat stroke
(D) all of the above

*Answer: C, Page: 45, Difficulty Level - M

3.20 You should use the back of your hand to assess the victim's relative:

(A) respiration rate
(B) skin temperature
(C) pulse rate
(D) oxygen level

*Answer: B, Page: 46, Difficulty Level - E

3.21 During the secondary survey, conduct a full-body assessment to check for:

(A) swelling
(B) bleeding
(C) deformity
(D) all of the above

*Answer: D, Page: 47, Difficulty Level - M

3.22 The victim's vital signs should be taken:

(A) during the primary survey
(B) during the secondary survey
(C) after a full-body assessment
(D) after the primary and secondary surveys

*Answer: A, Page: 47, Difficulty Level - M

3.23 During the secondary survey, which one of the following approaches would detect crepitus?

(A) looking
(B) listening
(C) feeling
(D) smelling

*Answer: B, Page: 47, Difficulty Level – M

3.24 The extent of the secondary survey and the emergency care you give will depend on:

(A) how much training you have
(B) how much extra help you have
(C) how quickly the EMS system arrives
(D) how much the victim cooperates

*Answer: C, Page: 48, Difficulty Level - M

3.25 Never move the victim unnecessarily until you:

(A) have ruled out the possibility of neck or spinal injuries
(B) know the EMS system is on the way
(C) have finished the primary survey
(D) know the victim is not in pain

*Answer: A, Page: 47, Difficulty Level - M

3.26 When checking the victim's abdomen, palpate the four quadrants separately. If you suspect injury:

(A) feel that quadrant first
(B) feel that quadrant last
(C) do not touch that quadrant
(D) skip that portion of the survey

*Answer: B, Page: 50, Difficulty level - M

3.27 If cervical spine injury is a possibility, the back survey should be conducted by:

(A) laying the victim out straight on his/her stomach
(B) professionally trained medical personnel
(C) slipping your hand beneath the back without moving the victim
(D) none of the above

*Answer: C, Page: 50, Difficulty Level – M

3.28 When surveying the lower extremities, check the top of each foot for:

(A) bleeding
(B) tenderness
(C) abnormal position
(D) a pulse

*Answer: D, Page: 51, Difficulty Level - M

3.29 The secondary survey is:

(A) done to check internal injuries
(B) a psychological assessment of the victim
(C) a full-body assessment from head to toe
(D) done if you're not sure you covered everything during the primary survey

*Answer: C, Page: 52, Difficulty Level - E

TRUE / FALSE

3.30 You should take all appropriate safety precautions to protect yourself, bystanders and victims at the scene from further injury. You should never risk your own safety.

*Answer: True, Page: 39, Difficulty Level - M

3.31 To maintain control of the situation, you should keep your voice powerful and authoritative.

*Answer: False, Page: 39, Difficulty Level - M

3.32 Cyanosis is blueness from lack of oxygen.

*Answer: True, Page: 40, Difficulty Level - M

3.33 If the victim is unconscious, always assume spinal damage.

*Answer: True, Page: 40, Difficulty Level - M

3.34 If the victim is not breathing spontaneously, go for help immediately.

*Answer: False, Page: 41, Difficulty Level - M

3.35 The radial pulse is the pulse at the groove on either side of the neck.

*Answer: False, Page: 41, Difficulty Level - M

3.36 It is important to ask the question, "Tell me where it hurts", even if the injury is obvious.

*Answer: True, Page: 44, Difficulty Level - M

3.37 The normal resting pulse rate for an adult is forty to eighty beats per minute.

*Answer: False, Page: 45, Difficulty Level - E

3.38 After taking the pulse, keep it clear in your memory so you don't have to waste time writing it down.

*Answer: False, Page: 45, Difficulty Level - M

3.39 When taking a history, whenever possible, ask open-ended questions so you don't suggest answers to the victim.

*Answer: True, Page: 47, Difficulty Level – M

3.40 If the victim is unresponsive, seems confused or is a child, get a history by talking to friends or family members.

*Answer: True, Page: 47, Difficulty Level - E

CHAPTER FOUR
BASIC LIFE SUPPORT : ARTIFICIAL VENTILATION

MULTIPLE CHOICE

4.1 Which of the following is a sign or symptom of respiratory distress?

(A) clammy skin
(B) dizziness
(C) abnormal skin color
(D) all of the above

*Answer: B, Page: 57, Difficulty Level - M

4.2 Without oxygenated blood, the brain cells are the first to die, usually within:

(A) two to four minutes
(B) four to six minutes
(C) six to eight minutes
(D) eight to ten minutes

*Answer: B, Page: 57, Difficulty Level - C

4.3 Which of the following is the <u>first</u> step in basic life support assessment?

(A) activating the EMS system
(B) opening the airway
(C) determining unresponsiveness
(D) determining breathlessness

*Answer: C, Page: 58, Difficulty Level - M

4.4 To determine responsiveness, you should:

(A) take the victim's pulse
(B) tap the victim gently on the shoulder and ask loudly "are you okay?"
(C) gently shake the victim
(D) none of the above

*Answer: B, Page: 58, Difficulty Level - M

4.5 If an infant is unresponsive and you are alone, you should:

(A) activate the EMS system immediately
(B) quickly find someone else to help
(C) give emergency care until someone else can activate the EMS system
(D) give emergency care for one minute, then activate the EMS system

*Answer: D, Page 58, Difficulty Level - M

4.6 Ideally, what position should the victim be in when opening the airway?

(A) supine
(B) prone
(C) anatomical
(D) lateral recumbent

*Answer: A, Page: 58, Difficulty Level - M

4.7 You should open the airway using the jaw-thrust maneuver if:

(A) you suspect cervical spine injury
(B) you do not suspect cervical spine injury
(C) the head-tilt / chin-lift position is unsuccessful
(D) A or C

*Answer: D, Page: 59, Difficulty Level - M

4.8 If the victim is breathing, maintain an open airway by placing the victim in:

(A) recovery position
(B) supine position
(C) prone position
(D) lateral recumbent

*Answer: A, Page: 59, Difficulty Level – M

4.9 Whenever possible, the most efficient method of rescue breathing is:

(A) mouth to nose
(B) mouth to mouth
(C) mouth to stoma
(D) none of the above

*Answer: B, Page: 60, Difficulty Level – E

4.10 The most common cause of difficulty with ventilation is:

(A) improper positioning of the head and chin
(B) failing to get a tight mouth to mouth seal
(C) blowing too hard and fast
(D) forgetting to pinch the nostrils closed

*Answer: A, Page: 60, Difficulty Level - M

4.11 In artificial ventilation, give __________ initial slow breaths allowing for deflation between breaths.

(A) two
(B) three
(C) four

*Answer: A, Page: 61, Difficulty Level - E

4.12 When providing rescue breathing, continue:

(A) for approximately five minutes
(B) until the victim begins breathing spontaneously
(C) until you are relieved by emergency personnel
(D) B or C

*Answer: D, Page: 62, Difficulty Level – M

4.13 When providing mouth to nose ventilation, tilt the victim's head __________ with one hand and lift the lower jaw __________ with the other hand.

(A) forward, back
(B) forward, forward
(C) back, forward
(D) back, back

*Answer: C, Page: 62, Difficulty Level - C

4.14 During artificial ventilation, it is common to get air into the stomach. This is called:

(A) aspiration
(B) gastric distention
(C) hyperventilation
(D) none of the above

*Answer: B, Page: 63, Difficulty Level - M

4.15 Perform rescue breathing at the rate of approximately __________ breaths per minute.

(A) 10
(B) 12
(C) 14
(D) 16

*Answer: B, Page: 62, Difficulty Level - M

4.16 You should use mouth to nose ventilation when:

(A) you can't open the victim's mouth
(B) the victim has no teeth
(C) the victim has mouth injuries
(D) all of the above

*Answer: D, Page: 62, Difficulty Level – M

4.17 When performing ventilation procedures on an infant, use your mouth to cover the:

(A) nose
(B) mouth
(C) mouth and nose

*Answer: C, Page: 64, Difficulty Level – E

4.18 The "look, listen, and feel" assessment method is used to establish:

(A) cervical spine injury
(B) responsiveness
(C) pulse
(D) breathlessness

*Answer: D, Page: 59, Difficulty Level - M

4.19 What is the first thing you should do in the case of complete airway obstruction?

(A) activate the EMS system
(B) begin the Heimlich maneuver
(C) encourage the victim to cough
(D) perform mouth to mouth ventilation

*Answer: A, Page: 65, Difficulty Level - M

4.20 If you suspect a person is choking you should first:

(A) perform rescue breathing
(B) perform the Heimlich maneuver
(C) perform firm back blows
(D) ask the victim, "Are you choking?"

*Answer: D, Page: 65, Difficulty Level – M

4.21 To perform the Heimlich maneuver on an unconscious person, place the person:

(A) in an upright position
(B) on his/her back
(C) on his/her side
(D) over the back of a chair

*Answer: B, Page: 66, Difficulty Level - E

4.22 When performing the Heimlich maneuver the thumb should be placed:

(A) slightly above the navel
(B) slightly above the xiphoid process
(C) over the sternum
(D) on the diaphragm

*Answer: A, Page: 66, Difficulty Level - M

4.23 Special variation of the Heimlich maneuver should be used on:

(A) pregnant victims
(B) infants
(C) obese victims
(D) all of the above

*Answer: D, Page: 67-68, Difficulty Level - M

4.24 The best indication of complete airway obstruction is:

(A) coughing
(B) inability to speak
(C) cyanosis
(D) clutching at the throat

*Answer: B, Page: 65, Difficulty Level - M

4.25 When performing the Heimlich maneuver on an obese or pregnant victim, place the fist:

(A) on the middle of the breastbone
(B) slightly above the navel
(C) near the margins of the rib cage
(D) none of the above

*Answer: A, Page: 67, Difficulty Level - C

4.26 If airway obstruction of an infant victim is caused by swelling, you should:

(A) use the finger sweep method
(B) perform rescue breathing
(C) transport the victim immediately to a medical facility
(D) deliver chest thrusts

*Answer: C, Page: 68, Difficulty Level - M

4.27 If the choking victim is a conscious infant, first you should do:

(A) chest thrusts
(B) back blows
(C) finger sweeps
(D) rescue breathing

*Answer: B, Page: 68, Difficulty Level - M

4.28 To perform chest trusts on an infant, position your fingers:

(A) between the nipples
(B) just above the naval
(C) slightly below the center of the nipples
(D) between the ribs

*Answer: C, Page: 69, Difficulty Level - C

4.29 The crucial first step of basic life support is:

(A) opening the airway
(B) rescue breathing
(C) chest compressions
(D) assessment

*Answer: D, Page: 69, Difficulty Level - M

TRUE / FALSE

4.30 By understanding the physiological process of breathing and methods of care, you can initiate and maintain an airway adequate enough to save most victims until emergency help arrives.

*Answer: True, Page: 56, Difficulty Level - M

4.31 If an adult victim is unresponsive and you are alone, give emergency care for two minutes and then activate the EMS system.

*Answer: False, Page: 58, Difficulty Level - M

4.32 A stoma is a surgical opening in the neck.

*Answer: True, Page: 62, Difficulty Level - E

4.33 When performing artificial ventilation you don't have to perform a head tilt on a victim with a stoma.

*Answer: True, Page: 62, Difficulty Level - M

4.34 Gastric distention occurs most often in children and airway-obstructed victims when breaths have been given too forcefully.

*Answer: True, Page: 63, Difficulty Level - M

4.35 The American Heart Association recommends pressing on the abdomen to relieve gastric distention.

*Answer: False, Page: 63, Difficulty Level - M

4.36 An high-pitched wheeze during inhalation is a sign of reduced air passage.

*Answer: True, Page: 65, Difficulty Level - M

4.37 The most common upper-airway obstruction in an unconscious victim is the tongue.

*Answer: True, Page: 64, Difficulty Level - E

4.38 If there is only partial airway obstruction, the victim will be able to cough.

*Answer: True, Page: 65, Difficulty Level - M

4.39 The Heimlich maneuver is an abdominal thrust delivered just below the sternum.

*Answer: False, Page: 65, Difficulty Level - M

CHAPTER FIVE
BASIC LIFE SUPPORT : CARDIOPULMONARY RESUSCITATION

MULTIPLE CHOICE

5.1 Cardiopulmonary resuscitation is:

(A) opening and maintaining the airway
(B) providing artificial ventilation through rescue breathing
(C) providing artificial circulation through chest compressions
(D) all of the above

*Answer: D, Page: 75, Difficulty Level - M

5.2 Which one of the following is the first step in the basic life support sequence?

(A) activate the EMS system
(B) determine unresponsiveness
(C) provide rescue breathing
(D) deliver chest compressions

*Answer: B, Page: 75, Difficulty Level - M

5.3 The best way to determine responsiveness is to:

(A) take the victim's pulse
(B) look, listen and feel
(C) ask loudly, "Are you okay?"
(D) check the victim's vital signs

*Answer: C, Page: 75, Difficulty Level - M

5.4 Choosing the method you will use to open the airway depends on:

(A) the victim's size
(B) whether you suspect cervical spine injury
(C) the equipment you have available
(D) all of the above

*Answer: B, Page: 77, Difficulty Level - E

5.5 After you have performed rescue breathing, assess the victim to determine:

(A) pulselessness
(B) airway obstruction
(C) cervical spine injury
(D) responsiveness

*Answer: A, Page: 77, Difficulty Level - M

5.6 To determine whether the heart is beating:

(A) take the victim's radial pulse
(B) use the look, listen and feel method
(C) deliver chest compressions
(D) take the victim's pulse at the carotid artery

*Answer: D, Page: 78, Difficulty Level - M

5.7 If you determine that the victim's heart is not beating, the next step in the basic life support sequence is to:

(A) activate the EMS system
(B) provide rescue breathing
(C) deliver chest compressions
(D) open the airway

*Answer: C, Page: 78, Difficulty Level - M

5.8 When delivering chest compressions, press straight down compressing the victim's sternum approximately:

(A) .5 to 1 inch
(B) 1 to 1.5 inches
(C) 1.5 to 2 inches
(D) 2 to 2.5 inches

*Answer: C, Page: 79, Difficulty Level - C

5.9 For an adult, chest compressions should be delivered at the rate of:

(A) 40 - 60 per minute
(B) 60 - 80 per minute
(C) 80 - 100 per minute
(D) over 100 per minute

*Answer: C, Page: 81, Difficulty Level - M

5.10 Proper position of the hands during CPR is critical. Placing hands too far to the right can:

(A) crack the sternum
(B) cause lacerations to the lung and liver
(C) break off the xiphoid process
(D) cause lacerations to the lung and heart

*Answer: B, Page: 80, Difficulty Level - M

5.11 When performing one-rescuer CPR, how many chest compressions should you deliver after each two rescue breaths?

(A) 10
(B) 15
(C) 20
(D) none of the above

*Answer: B, Page: 81, Difficulty Level - C

5.12 When performing two-rescuer CPR, CPR should continue at a rate of __________ compressions to __________ ventilation.

(A) 10, 2
(B) 15, 3
(C) 5, 1
(D) none of the above

*Answer: C, Page: 83, Difficulty Level - C

5.13 Which of the following would characterize unresponsiveness in an infant?

(A) no chest movements
(B) blue or pale skin
(C) no response when gently shaken or tapped
(D) all of the above

*Answer: D, Page: 86, Difficulty Level - M

5.14 In infants under one year of age, determine pulselessness:

(A) at the brachial pulse
(B) at the carotid pulse
(C) at the radial pulse
(D) none of the above

*Answer: A, Page: 86, Difficulty Level - M

5.15 In two rescuer CPR, the First Aider at the victim's side should deliver chest compressions and the First Aider at the victim's heard should:

(A) deliver the breaths
(B) maintain an open airway throughout resuscitation
(C) monitor the carotid pulse
(D) all of the above

*Answer: D, Page: 83, Difficulty Level - M

5.16 In two rescuer CPR, you should stop after the first minute to:

(A) rest
(B) change positions
(C) assess the carotid pulse
(D) activate the EMS system

*Answer: C, Page: 84, Difficulty Level - M

5.17 To determine unresponsiveness in an infant you should:

(A) shout
(B) shake the infant
(C) flick the soles' of the baby's feet
(D) A or C

*Answer: D, Page: 85, Difficulty Level - M

5.18 When performing chest compressions on an infant, how far should the lower sternum be depressed?

(A) .5 to 1 inch
(B) 1 to 1.5 inches
(C) 1.5 to 2 inches
(D) none of the above

*Answer: A, Page: 85, Difficulty Level - M

5.19 In delivering chest compressions to a child one to eight years old, use:

(A) two hands
(B) one hand
(C) the heel of one hand
(D) two fingers

*Answer: C, Page: 86, Difficulty Level - M

5.20 In infants to one year, deliver rescue breaths once every:

(A) two seconds
(B) three seconds
(C) four seconds
(D) five seconds

*Answer: B, Page: 86, Difficulty Level - M

5.21 What should you do if you think you have injured the victim during CPR?

(A) stop immediately
(B) continue performing CPR
(C) immediately treat the injury
(D) stop and wait for professional help

*Answer: B, Page: 86, Difficulty Level - M

5.22 Even properly performed CPR can cause complications. Which of the following might be a complication caused by CPR?

(A) lacerations to the liver
(B) hemothorax
(C) fractured rib
(D) all of the above

*Answer: D, Page: 88, Difficulty Level - M

5.23 The lower tip of the sternum is the:

(A) substernal notch
(B) xiphoid process
(C) clavicle
(D) none of the above

*Answer: B, Page: 79, Difficulty level – M

5.24 Under which of the following circumstances should you terminate CPR?

(A) breathing and heartbeat start again spontaneously
(B) you are exhausted and unable to continue life support
(C) another responsible or professional person assumes responsibility for basic life support
(D) any of the above

*Answer: D, Page: 82-83, Difficulty Level - M

5.25 If you are on duty or otherwise have a legal "duty to act", you are legally required to begin CPR on any victim who needs it unless:

(A) your certification has expired
(B) you don't have proper consent
(C) there are obviously fatal wounds
(D) you know the EMS system has been activated

*Answer: C, Page: 88, Difficulty Level - M

5.26 Research has shown that the key to survival of a cardiac arrest victim is:

(A) the degree of training the rescuer has
(B) early access to the victim, early CPR and early defibrillation by EMT's
(C) the victim's will to live
(D) proper assessment

*Answer: B, Page: 75, Difficulty Level - M

5.27 To determine breathlessness, you should:

(A) look, listen and feel
(B) palpitate the carotid artery
(C) perform mouth to mouth
(D) ask the victim to speak

*Answer: A, Page: 76, Difficulty Level - M

TRUE / FALSE

5.28 Cardiac arrest is a condition in which the heart stops beating.

*Answer: True, Page: 75, Difficulty Level - M

5.29 The shorter the time between cardiac arrest and the beginning of CPR, the great the victim's chance of survival.

*Answer: True, Page: 75, Difficulty Level - M

5.30 Retraining in CPR skills should occur yearly and recertification should occur every three to five years.

*Answer: False, Page: 75, Difficulty Level - C

5.31 You can cause serious medical complications to a victim if you deliver chest compressions while the heart is still beating.

*Answer: True, Page: 77, Difficulty Level - M

5.32 The carotid pulse is the first to cease when the heart stops beating.

*Answer: False, Page: 78, Difficulty Level - C

5.33 The point where the ribs are attached to the lower end of the sternum is the substernal notch.

*Answer: True, Page: 78, Difficulty Level - M

5.34 When delivering chest compressions, your elbows should be bent to keep from depressing the chest too much.

*Answer: False, Page: 78, Difficulty Level - M

5.35 Lift your hands off the chest between each compression to get enough force for the next compression.

*Answer: False, Page: 79, Difficulty Level - M

5.36 If your hands are positioned too high during CPR, you could crack the sternum.

*Answer: True, Page: 80, Difficulty Level - M

5.37 You should make sure that chest compressions last at least as long as release of the compression.

*Answer: True, Page: 82, Difficulty Level - M

5.38 Gasps, muscular contractions or seizure like convulsions might characterize unresponsiveness in an infant.

*Answer: True, Page: 86, Difficulty Level - M

5.39 In two-rescuer CPR, one should deliver both the rescue breaths and the chest compressions while the second person monitors the pulse.

*Answer: False, Page: 83, Difficulty Level - M

CHAPTER SIX
BLEEDING AND SHOCK

MULTIPLE CHOICE

6.1 When the body cannot compensate quickly enough for uncontrollable bleeding, the result is:

(A) cardiac arrest
(B) a heart attack
(C) unconsciousness
(D) shock

*Answer: D, Page: 93, Difficulty Level - M

6.2 Fatal shock can result from the loss of how much blood volume?

(A) 15 percent
(B) 20 percent
(C) 30 percent
(D) 40 percent

*Answer: C, Page: 93, Difficulty Level - C

6.3 The severity of bleeding depends on its source. The most difficult bleeding to control would come from:

(A) a vein
(B) an artery
(C) a capillary

*Answer: B, Page: 93, Difficulty Level - E

6.4 Blood coming from a vein would be what color?

(A) bright red
(B) dark bluish-red
(C) dark red
(D) dark brownish-red

*Answer: B, Page: 93, Difficulty Level - M

6.5 A hemophiliac is a person whose blood:

(A) is too thin
(B) lacks enough oxygen
(C) will not clot
(D) is low in iron

*Answer: C, Page: 93, Difficulty Level - M

6.6 The best method of controlling bleeding and the one you should try first is:

(A) indirect pressure
(B) elevation
(C) direct pressure
(D) tourniquet

*Answer: C, Page: 94, Difficulty Level - M

6.7 If the dressing becomes saturated with blood, what should you do?

(A) remove the dressing and replace it with a clean one
(B) put additional dressing over the top of the saturated one
(C) use a tourniquet
(D) none of the above

*Answer: B, Page: 96, Difficulty Level – M

6.8 You should elevate the bleeding part above the level of the heart unless you suspect:

(A) fracture
(B) dislocation
(C) spinal injury
(D) any of the above

*Answer: D, Page: 94, Difficulty Level - M

6.9 Indirect pressure is applied:

(A) at pressure points
(B) at the place where the blood is coming from
(C) directly above the bleeding wound
(D) none of the above

*Answer: A, Page: 97, Difficulty Level - M

6.10 The most commonly used arterial pressure points are the:

(A) temporal and maxillary
(B) carotid and radial
(C) femoral and carotid
(D) femoral and brachial

*Answer: D, Page: 97, Difficulty Level - C

6.11 The maxillary arterial pressure point is located:

(A) on each side of the neck next to the larynx
(B) on each side of the face on the inner surface of the lower jaw
(C) on each side of the groin
(D) on the inner arm just above the elbow

*Answer: B, Page: 99, Difficulty Level - M

6.12 Indirect pressure should be used:

(A) instead of direct pressure
(B) in addition to direct pressure
(C) as a last resort

*Answer: B, Page:97, Difficulty Level – M

6.13 All of the following are true statements concerning the use of tourniquets except:

(A) a tourniquet should only be used as a last resort
(B) you should loosen or remove a tourniquet just as soon as the bleeding stops
(C) a tourniquet can be improvised from a belt, handkerchief, or necktie
(D) a tourniquet can only be used on an extremity

*Answer: B, Page: 100, Difficulty Level – M

6.14 When treating victims of internal bleeding, first you should:

(A) secure and maintain an open airway
(B) activate the EMS system
(C) check for fractures
(D) position and treat for shock

*Answer: B, Page: 103, Difficulty Level - M

6.15 The best position for a victim with a nosebleed is:

(A) lying down
(B) sitting up with head tilted back
(C) sitting, leaning forward
(D) none of the above

*Answer: C, Page: 103, Difficulty Level – M

6.16 The loss of fluids and change in biochemical balance describes what type of shock?

(A) neurogenic
(B) septic
(C) psychogenic
(D) metabolic

*Answer: D, Page: 106, Difficulty Level - C

6.17 The cells most sensitive to a lack of oxygen are those in the heart, brain and lungs; they can be irreparably damaged in:

(A) two to four minutes
(B) four to six minutes
(C) six to eight minutes
(D) eight to ten minutes

*Answer: B, Page: 105, Difficulty Level - C

6.18 During what stage of shock does the body shunt blood away from the extremities and abdomen to the heart, brain and lungs?

(A) compensatory
(B) progressive
(C) irreversible

*Answer: C, Page: 106, Difficulty Level – M

6.19 Dull eyes, dilated pupils, and shallow irregular breathing are signs of what stage of shock?

(A) compensatory
(B) progressive
(C) irreversible

*Answer: C, Page; 106, Difficulty Level – M

6.20 You can prevent shock by:

(A) controlling bleeding
(B) splinting and immobilizing fractures
(C) loosening restrictive clothing
(D) all of the above

*Answer: D, Page: 109, Difficulty Level – M

6.21 The best position for an unconscious victim of shock is:

(A) supine
(B) supine with feet elevated
(C) on his or her side
(D) none of the above

*Answer: C, Page:109, Difficulty Level – M

6.22 For a victim of shock, normally the lower extremities should be elevated to help:

(A) make the victim more comfortable
(B) reduce blood in the extremities
(C) immobilize fractures
(D) make breathing easier

*Answer: B, Page:109, Difficulty Level – M

6.23 Anaphylactic shock is caused by:

(A) as intense allergic reaction
(B) toxins from severe infection
(C) a loss of blood
(D) a change in biochemical balance

*Answer: A, Page:109, Difficulty Level – M

6.24 Which one of the following factors would <u>not</u> influence the severity of shock?

(A) sex
(B) age
(C) pregnancy
(D) physical condition

*Answer: A, Page:105, Difficulty Level – E

6.25 Which of the following statements about children and shock is <u>not</u> true?

(A) A child may go from no sign of shock to irreversible shock very suddenly.
(B) Shock in a child generally develops early and progresses rapidly.
(C) For children in shock, always begin emergency care very early.
(D) With children, treat shock as signs and symptoms appear.

*Answer: D, Page: 106, Difficulty Level – M

6.26 In managing shock, after activating the EMS system, what should you do next?

(A) control bleeding
(B) elevate lower extremities
(C) secure an open airway
(D) splint any fractures

*Answer: C, Page:106, Difficulty Level – M

6.27 As a rule, anaphylactic reactions occur more frequently and rapidly when the antigen is:

(A) injected
(B) Ingested
(C) Inhaled

*Answer: A, Page:111, Difficulty Level – M

6.28 If anaphylactic shock is due to an insect sting, you should:

(A) elevate the affected area
(B) place a constriction band between the sting site and the heart
(C) apply pressure to the area
(D) none of the above

*Answer: B, Page: 112, Difficulty Level - E

6.29 Which of the following signs of anaphylactic shock would most likely lead to circulatory collapse?

(A) cyanosis
(B) tightness or pain in the chest
(C) coughing, hoarseness
(D) weak or imperceptible pulse

*Answer: D, Page: 111, Difficulty Level - C

TRUE / FALSE

6.30 The loss of three pints of blood in an adult can be fatal if it occurs over the course of a few hours.

*Answer: True, Page: 92, Difficulty Level - M

6.31 All the body processes are affected by shock.

*Answer: True, Page: 92, Difficulty Level – M

6.32 A place where an artery is close to the skin surface and lies over a bone is a pressure point.

*Answer: True, Page:97, Difficulty Level - M

6.33 Pressure points should be used with caution because indirect pressure can cause damage from inadequate blood flow.

*Answer: True, Page: 97, Difficulty Level - M

6.34 If you use an air splint to control bleeding, deflate it as soon as the bleeding has stopped.

*Answer: False, Page: 100, Difficulty Level – M

6.35 Using a tourniquet almost guarantees that the extremity below the tourniquet will have to be amputated.

*Answer: True, Page: 100, Difficulty Level – M

6.36 The signs and symptoms of internal bleeding are similar to those of shock.

*Answer: True, Page: 101, Difficulty Level – M

6. 37 Internal bleeding may not cause signs or symptoms for hours or even days.

*Answer: True, Page:102, Difficulty Level – M

6.38 Even severe nosebleeds seldom cause enough blood loss to cause shock.

*Answer: False, Page: 103, Difficulty Level - M

6.39 Shock is the collapse and progressive failure of the cardiovascular system.

*Answer: True, Page: 104, Difficulty Level - M

CHAPTER SEVEN
SOFT - TISSUE INJURIES

MULTIPLE CHOICE

7.1 The internal bleeding that results from a __________ can be severe enough to cause shock:

(A) contusion
(B) hematoma
(C) crush injury
(D) wound

*Answer: C, Page: 119, Difficulty Level - M

7.2 Contusions, hematoma and crush injuries are all types of:

(A) closed injuries
(B) bruises
(C) fractures
(D) lacerations

*Answer: A, Page: 119, Difficulty Level - M

7.3 A collection of blood beneath the skin is called a:

(A) hematoma
(B) contusion
(C) bruise
(D) closed wound

*Answer: A, Page: 119, Difficulty Level - E

7.4 To help reduce the swelling and relieve the pain from a bruise, you should use:

(A) pressure
(B) a warm compress
(C) ice
(D) a splint

*Answer: C, Page: 119, Difficulty Level - M

7.5 An open wound caused by rubbing and scraping off layers of skin is:

(A) a laceration
(B) an abrasion
(C) an avulsion
(D) a puncture

*Answer: B, Page: 120, Difficulty Level - E

7.6 The most serious threat from abrasions is:

(A) shock
(B) external bleeding
(C) internal bleeding
(D) contamination or infection

*Answer: D, Page: 120, Difficulty Level - M

7.7 Open wounds characterized by sharp, even cuts with smooth edges are:

(A) linear lacerations
(B) stellate lacerations
(C) avulsions
(D) punctures

*Answer: A, Page: 121, Difficulty Level - M

7.8 The greatest danger with linear lacerations is:

(A) shock
(B) internal bleeding
(C) infection
(D) damage to tendons and nerves

*Answer: D, Page: 121, Difficulty Level - M

7.9 When a gunshot wound causes both entrance and exit wounds, the entrance wound is generally _________ the exit wound.

(A) smaller than
(B) larger than
(C) similar in size to

*Answer: A, Page: 122, Difficulty Level - M

7.10 For victim of crush inuuries, you shoul always suspect:

(A) hidden external bleeding
(B) extreme pain
(C) internal damage
(D) shock

*Answer: C, Page: 123, Difficulty Level - M

7.11 Complications such as cellulitis, hepatitis and tetnus would most likely result from:

(A) a snake bite
(B) a dog bite
(C) a puncture wound
(D) amputation

*Answer: B, Page: 123, Difficulty Level - M

7.12 Because of the high infection rate, the most difficult bite to manage is a:

(A) dog bite
(B) snake bite
(C) human bite

*Answer: C, Page: 124, Difficulty Level - E

7.13 Under what conditions should you activate the EMS system?

(A) if a wound has spurted blood
(B) if a wound is deeper than the outer layer of skin
(C) if there is embedded debris
(D) any of the above

*Answer: D, Page: 125, Difficulty Level - M

7.14 The tearing loose of a flap of kin is:

(A) a laceration
(B) an incision
(C) an avulsion
(D) a puncture

*Answer: C, Page: 121, Difficulty Level - M

7.15 Stellate lacerations differ from linear lacerations in that stellate lacerations:

(A) bleed much more
(B) carry more infection
(C) produce a ragged incision
(D) are usually deeper

*Answer: C, Page: 121, Difficulty Level - M

7.16 Because there is a high chance of contact with the victim's blood ro body fluids when treating soft-tissue injuries, you should:

(A) wear latex gloves when possible
(B) take measures that provide body-substance isolation
(C) wash your hands thoroughly after contact with the victim
(D) all of the above

*Answer: D, Page: 125, Difficulty Level – E

7.17 An "occlusive" dressing would be one that is:

(A) sanitary
(B) absorbent
(C) airtight
(D) moist

*Answer: C, Page:127, Difficulty Level – M

7.18 If organs are protruding through an open abdominal wound, what should you do?

(A) try to replace the organ back into the abdomen
(B) cover the protruding organ with an absorbent cotton dressing
(C) moisten a sterile dressing and cover the wounds
(D) all of the above

*Answer: C, Page:127, Difficulty Level – M

7.19 When dressing a wound from a penetrating chest injury:

(A) tape down all sides to prevent infection
(B) use a material that allows air to circulate
(C) tape down the dressing on three sides, leave one corner untaped
(D) A and B

*Answer: C, Page: 127, Difficulty Level – C

7.20 The only time an impaled object should be removed in the field is if:

(A) it interferes with chest compressions
(B) it penetrates the cheek
(C) it is causing unbearable pain
(D) A or B

*Answer: D, Page:127, Difficulty Level – M

7.21 Bleeding from an impaled object wound should be controlled with:

(A) indirect pressure
(B) direct pressure
(C) pressure on the impaled object
(D) a tourniquet

*Answer: B, Page:127, Difficulty Level – M

7.22 An impaled object should be secured manually to prevent:

(A) infection
(B) bleeding
(C) movement
(D) pain

*Answer: C, Page:127, Difficulty Level – M

7.23 To remove an impaled object in the cheek, <u>first</u> you should:

(A) activate the EMS system
(B) clean the area to prevent infection
(C) feel inside the victim's mouth to determine penetration
(D) remove the object in the direction in which it entered

*Answer: C, Page:128, Difficulty Level – C

7.24 When treating a puncture wound from an impaled object you should:

(A) remove the object immediately
(B) stabilize the object as much as possible
(C) shorten the object if possible
(D) apply slight pressure on the object

*Answer: 127, Page: 127, Difficulty Level – M

7.25 Which of the following would come <u>first</u> in the sequence of emergency care for an impaled object injury?

(A) remove clothing to expose the wound
(B) activate the EMS system
(C) control bleeding
(D) stabilize the object

*Answer: A, Page:127, Difficulty Level – C

7.26 Which of the following statements about emergency care of amputations is <u>not</u> true?

(A) generally you should not waste time looking for amputated parts
(B) wrap the amputated part is a plastic or foil wrap, then put it in a bag
(C) place the wrapped and bagged part on dry ice or freeze it
(D) all statements are true

*Answer: C, Page: 128, Difficulty Level – M

7.27 Most clamping injuries involve:

(A) feet
(B) legs
(C) arms
(D) fingers

*Answer: D, Page: 128, Difficulty Level – M

7.28 Which of the following statements is <u>not</u> true concerning clamping injuries and their treatment?

(A) You should not try to remove the clamping object without activating the EMS system first.
(B) You should remove the clamping object as soon as possible.
(C) If possible, you should elevate the affected extremity.
(D) The longer the tissue is in the clamping object, the more severe the swellling will be.

*Answer: A, Page:128, Difficulty Level – M

7.29 The greatest threat from an avulsion wound is:

(A) infection
(B) bleeding
(C) lack of circulation
(D) damaged nerves and tendons

*Answer:C, Page:129, Difficulty Level – M

TRUE / FALSE

7.30 Soft-tissue injuries are often the most obvious and dramatic and usually the most serious type of injury

*Answer: False, Page: 129, Difficulty Level – M

7.31 A traumatically caused injury that disrupts the normal continuity of the tissue, organ or bone affected is a wound.

*Answer: True, Page: 118, Difficulty Level – M

7.32 In a contusion, the dermis remains intact but there is damage to the epidermis layer.

*Answer: False, Page: 119, Difficulty Level – C

7.33 A hematoma is a collection of blood beneath the skin>

*Answer: True, Page: 119, Difficulty Level – M

7.34 Linear lacerations generally heal better than stellate lacerations.

*Answer: True, Page: 121, Difficulty Level – M

7.35 Because knife wounds are easy to see, first aiders too frequently concentrate only on the superficial skin wound and fail to consider the underlying damage to organs.

*Answer: True, Page:122, Difficulty Level – M

7.36 A bite wound is actually a combination of a contusion and a laceration.

*Answer: False, Page: 123, Difficulty Level – M

7.37 The way you handle an amputated part can determine whether if can be reattached later by a surgeon.

*Answer: True, Page: 128, Difficulty Level – E

7.38 When attempting to preserve an amputated part, keep it as warm and moist as possible.

*Answer: False, Page: 128, Difficulty Level – M

7.39 The longer the tissue remains in a clamping object, the more difficult it becomes to remove it.

*Answer: True, Page: 128, Difficulty Level – M

7.40 If possible, you should rinse off an amputated part with water.

*Answer: True, Page: 128, Difficulty Level - M

CHAPTER EIGHT
INJURIES TO THE FACE, EYE, AND THROAT

MULTIPLE CHOICE

8.1 When assessing an eye injury, you should suspect significant damage if the victim:

(A) has loss of vision that does not improve when he or she blinks
(B) loses part of the field of vision
(C) has double vision
(D) any of the above

*Answer: D, Page: 135, Difficulty Level - M

8.2 If an object becomes lodged in the eyeball you should:

(A) carefully remove it with a cotton swab
(B) put a bandage compress over both eyes and activate the EMS system
(C) flush the eye with water
(D) draw the upper lid over the lower lid

*Answer: B, Page: 136, Difficulty Level - M

8.3 A loss of sensation over the eyebrow, profuse nasal discharge and a paralysis of upward gaze are all signs and symptoms of:

(A) ecchymosis
(B) progressing blindness
(C) orbital fracture
(D) none of the above

*Answer: C, Page: 136-137, Difficulty Level - M

8.4 If you suspect injury to the eyeball from an orbital fracture you should:

(A) use ice packs on the injured eye
(B) keep the victim in sitting position
(C) keep the victim in supine position
(D) none of the above

*Answer: C, Page: 137, Difficulty Level - C

8.5 If you see a pear-shaped eyeball or blood in the front chamber of the eye, you would suspect injury to the:

(A) orbit
(B) globe
(C) conjunctiva

*Answer: B, Page: 138, Difficulty Level - C

8.6 In treating injuries to the globe you should:

(A) apply light pressure with a light sterile dressing
(B) patch only the injured eye
(C) keep the victim in sitting position
(D) patch both eyes

*Answer: D, Page: 138, Difficulty Level - M

8.7 In which eye-emergency situation should you activate the EMS system?

(A) orbital fracture
(B) injury to the globe
(C) chemical burn to the eye
(D) all of the above

*Answer: D, Page: 137-138, Difficulty Level - M

8.8 With a chemical burn to the eye, you should continuously irrigate the eye with running water for at least:

(A) 10 - 15 minutes
(B) 15 - 20 minutes
(C) 20 - 30 minutes
(D) 30 - 60 minutes

*Answer: D, Page: 138, Difficulty Level - M

8.9 Impaled or embedded objects should be removed:

(A) as quickly as possible
(B) only after activating the EMS system
(C) only by a physician
(D) only if there is profuse bleeding

*Answer: C, Page: 139, Difficulty Level - M

8.10 Which of the following best describes emergency care procedures for eye injuries from an impaled object:

(A) remove the object, then bandage and dress the eye
(B) secure a protective cone over the object with a thick dressing and bandage both eyes
(C) stabilize the object by applying slight pressure with a heavy dressing
(D) remove the object and apply direct pressure to control bleeding

*Answer: B, Page: 140, Difficulty Level - C

8.11 Which one of the following would be correct procedure for general emergency care of eye injuries?

(A) removing any blood or blood clots from the eye
(B) applying salves or medicines to the injured eye
(C) giving the victim only liquids by mouth
(D) limiting use of the uninjured eye

*Answer: D, Page: 135, Difficulty Level - M

8.12 In most eye injury cases, you should patch:

(A) only the injured eye
(B) only the uninjured eye
(C) both eyes
(D) neither eye

*Answer: C, Page: 135, Difficulty Level - M

8.13 Generally speaking, when should you remove a contact lens from an injured eye?

(A) when there is a chemical burn
(B) when the eyelid in injured
(C) when the globe is injured
(D) all of the above

*Answer: A, Page: 140, Difficulty Level - M

8.14 In victims with trauma to the face, mouth and jaw, you should suspect:

(A) extensive bleeding
(B) cervical spine and spinal injuries
(C) blocked air passages
(D) shock

*Answer: B, Page: 142, Difficulty Level - C

8.15 The only time you should irrigate an injured eye is in the case of:

(A) an injured eyeball
(B) an object embedded in the eye
(C) a chemical burn
(D) all eye injures should be irrigated

*Answer: C, Page: 139, Difficulty Level - M

8.16 The white part of the eye is called the:

(A) sclera
(B) orbit
(C) conjunctiva
(D) globe

*Answer: A, Page: 141, Difficulty Level - M

8.17 What is the <u>first</u> thing you should do in treating injures to the face?

(A) control hemorrhage
(B) establish an airway
(C) immobilize the neck
(D) cover exposed nerves, tendons and blood vessels with a moist sterile dressing

*Answer: B, Page: 142, Difficulty Level - M

8.18 When caring for injures to the mouth and jaw, examine the mouth for:

(A) broken or missing teeth
(B) bleeding
(C) injury to the tongue
(D) none of the above

*Answer: A, Page: 142, Difficulty Level - M

8.19 In attempting to save a tooth for reimplantation you should:

(A) wrap the tooth in dry gauze
(B) scrub the tooth to remove any debris
(C) wrap the tooth in moist gauze
(D) only handle the tooth at the root

*Answer: C, Page: 142, Difficulty Level - M

8.20 Dentures should be left in if they are:

(A) broken
(B) unbroken
(C) A & B

*Answer: B, Page: 142, Difficulty Level - M

8.21 A sign and symptom of facial fracture would be:

(A) bleeding from the nose and mouth
(B) numbness or pain
(C) the distance between the eyes appears too wide
(D) all of the above

*Answer: D, Page: 142, Difficulty Level - M

8.22 Drooling, difficult speech and pain around the ears are all signs of:

(A) maxilla fracture
(B) mandible fracture
(C) nasal fracture
(D) malar fracture

*Answer: B, Page: 142, Difficulty Level - C

8.23 What is the first priority in caring for a victim of maxillofacial fracture?

(A) activating the EMS system
(B) controlling bleeding
(C) establishing and maintaining the airway
(D) stabilizing the neck

*Answer: C, Page: 142, Difficulty Level - M

8.24 if you suspect lower jaw fracture, carefully immobilize the lower jaw unless:

(A) there is considerable bleeding in the mouth
(B) there are missing teeth
(C) there is vomiting
(D) you suspect spinal injury

*Answer: A, Page: 144, Difficulty Level - M

8.25 The only time you should try to remove an impaled object from the cheek is:

(A) when penetration is all the way through
(B) when the object is loose
(C) when there is a threat to airway obstruction
(D) when all of the above conditions are present

*Answer: D, Page: 143, Difficulty Level - M

8.26 the most common type of facial fractures are:

(A) mandible
(B) nasal
(C) malar
(D) maxilla

*Answer: B, Page: 146, Difficulty Level - M

8.27 Which one of the following would be correct for treatment of injury to the ear?

(A) pack the ear to stop bleeding
(B) probe the ear to determine any inner ear damage
(C) treat as you would for other soft-tissue injuries
(D) remove any objects logged in the ear

*Answer: C, Page: 146, Difficulty Level - M

8.28 Clear or bloody fluid draining from the ear can indicate:
(A) loss of hearing
(B) a foreign object lodged inside
(C) skull fracture

*Answer: C, Page: 146, Difficulty Level - M

8.29 When treating a throat injury, you should keep the victim lying down to:

(A) control bleeding
(B) prevent spinal damage
(C) lessen the chance of air entering the blood vessels
(D) make the victim comfortable

*Answer: C, Page; 147, Difficulty Level - C

8.30 A victim of a throat injury should be placed in what position?

(A) supine
(B) on his or her left side
(C) on his or her right side
(D) at a 45 degree angle

*Answer: B, Page: 147, Difficulty Level - C

TRUE / FALSE

8.31 Approximately 75 percent of all victims involved in motor vehicle accidents sustain at least minor facial trauma.

*Answer: True, Page: 134, Difficulty Level - E

8.32 Nearly twenty percent of all serious eye injuries occur in or around the home.

*Answer: False, Page: 135, Difficulty Level - M

8.33 Whenever the orbit has been fractured, you should assume there is also head injury.

*Answer: True, Page: 137, Difficulty Level - M

8.34 If an eye injury involves the eyeball itself, use light pressure to control bleeding.

*Answer: False, Page: 137, Difficulty Level - M

8.35 The first ten minutes following a chemical burn to the eye often determine the final outcome of the injury.

*Answer: True, Page: 138, Difficulty Level - M

8.36 When irrigating an eye, pour from the inside corner, across the eyeball to the outside edge.

*Answer: True, Page: 138, Difficulty Level - M

8.37 The next best irrigant to water for treating eyes is diluted vinegar.

*Answer: False, Page: 139, Difficulty Level - M

8.38 If the victim is wearing glasses you can rule out the possibility of contact lenses.

*Answer: False, Page: 140, Difficulty Level - M

8.39 Signs and symptoms indicating maxilla fracture would include black eyes, nosebleed, and numbness of the upper cheek.

*Answer: True, Page: 142, Difficulty Level - M

8.40 In almost all facial injury cases, the first concern should be to control bleeding.

*Answer: False, Page: 142, Difficulty Level – M

8.41 A tooth can usually be successfully reimplanted if it is inserted back into the socket within 30 minutes.

*Answer: True, Page: 149, Difficulty Level - M

CHAPTER NINE
INJURIES TO THE CHEST, ABDOMEN, AND GENITALIA

MULTIPLE CHOICE

9.1 Which one of the following statements about chest injuries is <u>not</u> true.

(A) All chest trauma should be considered life threatening until proven otherwise.
(B) Chest injury is the number one leading cause of death from trauma.
(C) Victims of chest injury can look fine but deteriorate suddenly.
(D) You should always assume cardiac damage with a chest injury until it is ruled out.

Answer: B, Page: 154, Difficulty Level - M

9.2 Two of the most important signs of chest injury are:
(A) coughing up blood and cyanosis
(B) weak pulse and shock
(C) tracheal deviation and cyanosis
(D) changes in normal breathing patterns and the respiratory rate

*Answer: D, Page: 155, Difficulty Level - M

9.3 A shortness of breath or difficulty in breathing is:

(A) dyspnea
(B) cyanosis
(C) hemoptysis
(D) paradoxical breathing

*Answer: A, Page: 155, Difficulty Level - M

9.4 If a victim breathes more than __________ times in a minute, there is probably chest injury.

(A) 20
(B) 24
(C) 30
(D) 36

*Answer: B, Page: 155, Difficulty Level - C

9.5 Your first priority in caring for a victim with a chest injury is to:

(A) control bleeding
(B) remove any impaled objects
(C) treat for shock
(D) ensure adequate ventilation

*Answer: D, Page: 155, Difficulty Level - M

9.6 If an object is impaled in the chest, you should:

(A) shorten the object as much as possible
(B) remove the object
(C) stabilize the object and leave it
(D) none of the above

*Answer: C, Page: 156, Difficulty Level - M

9.7 To check for flail chest, watch for:

(A) discoloration of the head, neck and shoulders
(B) bulging neck veins
(C) a see-saw motion as the victim breathes
(D) bloodshot eyes

*Answer: C, Page: 157, Difficulty Level - C

9.8 A condition in which the sides of the chest move opposite each other during breathing is called:

(A) paradoxical breathing
(B) crepitus
(C) traumatic asphyxia
(D) dyspnea

*Answer: A, Page: 157, Difficulty Level - M

9.9 You should stabilize flail chest by applying:

(A) direct pressure
(B) a pillow or bulky dressing
(C) a splint to the chest
(D) none of the above

*Answer: B, Page: 157, Difficulty Level – M

9.10 A sudden compression of the chest wall that forces blood the wrong way out of the heart is:

(A) pneumothorax
(B) crepitus
(C) traumatic asphyxia
(D) none of the above

*Answer: C, Page: 157, Difficulty Level - M

9.11 The most common symptom of rib fracture is:

(A) bleeding
(B) labored breathing
(C) obvious deformity
(D) pain

*Answer: D, Page: 158, Difficulty Level - M

9.12 The top priority in caring for broken ribs is making sure the victim can breathe adequately by:

(A) splinting the chest
(B) performing mouth to mouth
(C) placing the victim in supine position
(D) none of the above

*Answer: A, Page: 158, Difficulty Level - M

9.13 Which of the following should you avoid doing when caring for a victim with broken ribs?

(A) taping the ribs
(B) using continuous strapping
(C) wrapping the victim's chest if the ribs are depressed or there is frothy blood coming from the mouth
(D) all of the above

*Answer: B, Page: 159, Difficulty Level - M

9.14 One of the few emergencies in which seconds strictly count is:

(A) hemothorax
(B) tension pneumothorax
(C) open pneumothorax
(D) pneumothorax

*Answer: B, Page: 160, Difficulty Level - M

9.15 A condition in which air from a lung or from the outside fills the chest cavity, but does not fill the lung is called:

(A) hemothorax
(B) tension pneumothorax
(C) open pneumothorax
(D) pneumothorax

*Answer: D, Page: 161, Difficulty Level - M

9.16 A sudden, sharp chest pain and failure of the lung to expand during inhalation are signs of:

(A) hemothorax
(B) tension pneumothorax
(C) open pneumothorax
(D) pneumothorax

*Answer: D, Page: 161, Difficulty Level - C

9.17 In caring for a victim with tension pneumothorax, it is important to remember to:

(A) control external bleeding
(B) leave one corner of a chest bandage untapped
(C) apply an occlusive dressing to create an airtight seal
(D) keep the victim upright at all times

*Answer: B, Page: 161, Difficulty Level - M

9.18 Which one of the following signs and symptoms would a victim of hemothorax most likely display:

(A) failure of the lung to expand during inhalation
(B) bulging of neck veins
(C) rapid heart beat
(D) moist sucking or bubbling sounds as air passes in and out of the wound

*Answer: C, Page: 161, Difficulty Level - C

9.19 If a victim has suffered abdominal trauma, until proven otherwise, you should also assume that he or she has suffered:

(A) multiple fractures
(B) chest trauma
(C) cervical spine damage
(D) all of the above

*Answer: B, Page: 163, Difficulty Level - M

9.20 Closed abdominal wounds may be extremely dangerous because of:

(A) loss of blood
(B) injury to internal organs
(C) infection
(D) all of the above

*Answer: B, Page: 164, Difficulty Level - M

9.21 When assessing a victim for abdominal injury, gently palpate all four quadrants watching for:

(A) guarding
(B) rigidity
(C) pain
(D) all of the above

*Answer: D, Page: 164, Difficulty Level - M

9.22 Usually, the most comfortable position for victims with abdominal injuries is:

(A) sitting upright
(B) on their back with head elevated
(C) on their side in fetal position
(D) on their back with knees flexed

*Answer: D, Page: 165, Difficulty Level - M

9.23 Abdominal contents protruding through a laceration or other wound is called:

(A) hernia
(B) evisceration
(C) impalement
(D) abdominal trauma

*Answer: B, Page: 165, Difficulty Level - M

9.24 In preserving the chain of evidence of a victim of sexual assault, <u>do not</u>:

(A) allow her to bathe or douche
(B) clean wounds if possible
(C) put objects with blood on them in plastic bags
(D) all of the above

*Answer: C, Page: 167, Difficulty Level - M

9.25 In treating injuries to the genitalia, it is important to:

(A) find out how the injury happened
(B) protect the victim's rights
(C) protect the victim's privacy
(D) get proper consent

*Answer: C, Page: 167, Difficulty Level - M

TRUE / FALSE

9.26 The most visually disturbing or alarming chest injuries are usually the most life-threatening as well.

*Answer: False, Page: 155, Difficulty Level - M

9.27 Flail chest is a life-threatening injury because it involves bruising of the lung tissue and inadequate oxygenation of the heart.

*Answer: True, Page: 157, Difficulty Level - C

9.28 While broke ribs themselves are not life-threatening, they can cause injuries that are.

*Answer: True, Page: 158, Difficulty Level - M

9.29 Pneumothorax is a condition in which blood fills the chest cavity.

*Answer: False, Page: 161, Difficulty Level - M

9.30 The organs most frequently damaged by penetrating abdominal trauma are the liver, small intestine and colon.

*Answer: True, Page: 163, Difficulty Level - C

9.31 If abdominal contents are protruding through a wound, never touch them or try to replace them in the abdominal cavity.

*Answer: True, Page: 165, Difficulty Level - M

9.32 Injuries to the external male genitalia are excruciatingly painful and usually life-threatening.

*Answer: False, Page: 167, Difficulty Level - E

CHAPTER TEN
BANDAGING

MULTIPLE CHOICE

10.1 Which one of the following is not included in the four basic purpose for dressings and bandages?

(A) control pain
(B) immobilize the wound site
(C) keep the wound dry
(D) prevent further contamination and injury

*Answer: A, Page: 172, Difficulty Level - M

10.2 The definition of Aseptic according to Chapter 10 is:

(A) all microorganisms have been killed
(B) free of bacteria
(C) all spores have been killed
(D) all of the above

*Answer: B, Page: 173, Difficulty Level - M

10.3 In an emergency, you can use any of the following as dressings except for:

(A) clean handkerchiefs
(B) towels
(C) sanitary napkins
(D) toilet tissue

*Answer: D, Page: 173, Difficulty Level - M

10.4 A universal dressing is:

(A) plastic wrap, aluminum foil, petroleum gauze, or other dressing that forms an airtight seal
(B) sterile gauze saturated with petroleum to keep it from sticking to a wound
(C) a dressing made from a nine by thirty-six inch piece of thick, absorbent material
(D) none of the above

*Answer: C, Page: 174, Difficulty Level - M

10.5 Which one of the following dressings is referred to as multi-trauma dressings, trauma packs, general-purpose dressings, burn pads, or ABD dressings.

(A) bandage compresses
(B) gauze pads
(C) special pads
(D) none of the above

*Answer: C, Page: 174, Difficulty Level - M

10.6 Which one of the following is <u>not</u> a sign that a bandage is too tight?

(A) the skin below the bandage (distal) is tingling or numb
(B) the skin below the bandage (distal) is warm to the touch
(C) the skin around the bandage becomes pale or cyanotic
(D) the victim complains of pain, usually only a few minutes after bandage is applied

*Answer: B, Page: 175, Difficulty Level - M

10.7 A cravat bandage is made by:

(A) cutting along the diagonal fold of a 40 inch square piece of unbleached cotton cloth
(B) make a one-inch fold along the base of a triangular bandage, then, bringing the point to the center of the folded base, placing it underneath the fold
(C) sealing gauze pads over a wound by wrapping a roller bandage around the wound site
(D) any of the above

*Answer: B, Page: 165, Difficulty Level - M

10.8 The use of two gauze rolls, wrapped alternately around and across the wound until it is wrapped completely is an example of:

(A) roller bandages
(B) cravat bandages
(C) triangular bandages
(D) none of the above

*Answer: A, Page; 176, Difficulty Level – E

10.9 Which one of the following is not a true principle of dressing and bandaging?

(A) ask the victim how the bandage feels; if it's too tight, loosen it and make it comfortable but snug
(B) bandages should not be too loose; neither dressing nor the bandage should shift or slip
(C) the original dressing should be removed and replaced if blood soaks through
(D) the body part should be bandaged in the position in which it is to remain

*Answer: B, Page: 178, Difficulty Level - M

10.10 The use of an elastic roller bandage is not encouraged except in cases of:

(A) shock
(B) profuse bleeding
(C) fracture
(D) none of the above

*Answer: B, Page: 176, Difficulty Level - M

10.11 Which one of the following is considered the most popular and easy to use roller bandage?

(A) nonelastic, self-adhering
(B) gauze rolls
(C) elastic
(D) none of the above

*Answer: A, Page; 176, Difficulty Level - M

10.12 When bandaging over a joint, the joint should be bandaged in:

(A) the position that holds the wound closed
(B) a straightened position
(C) the position in which the joint is to remain
(D) a bent position

*Answer: C, Page: 178, Difficulty Level – M

10.13 Material used for dressings should be as __________ as possible.

(A) strong
(B) thick
(C) clean
(D) snug

*Answer: C, Page: 178, Difficulty Level - E

10.14 When applying a bandage, it should cover which one of the following?

(A) the entire wound
(B) the full length of the extremity
(C) the splint
(D) the entire dressing

*Answer: D, Page: 178, Difficulty Level - E

10.15 A cravat may be used in the bandaging of:

(A) an ear
(B) the jaw or cheek
(C) a leg
(D) none of the above
(E) all of the above

*Answer: E, Page: 181, Difficulty Level - E

10.16 A triangular bandage may be used for which of the following:

(A) the chest or back
(B) to make a cravat
(C) the hip
(D) to make sling
(E) all of the above

*Answer: E, Page: 179-180, Difficulty Level – E

10.17 An occlusive dressing is best described by which one of the following:

(A) a gauze pad
(B) an airtight dressing
(C) a sterile dressing
(D) an aseptic dressing

*Answer: B, Page 182, Difficulty Level - M

TRUE / FALSE

10.18 A wound should be dressed and bandaged as quickly as possible to control heavy hemorrhaging.

*Answer: False, Page: 172, Difficulty Level - M

10.19 Improper wound care can result in the loss of a limb.

*Answer: True, Page: 172, Difficulty Level - M

10.20 A bandage is a sterile covering for a wound.

*Answer: False, Page: 173, Difficulty Level - E

10.21 The ideal dressing is layered, consists of course mesh gauze, and is bulky enough to immobilize tissues and protect the wound.

*Answer: True, Page: 173, Difficulty Level - M

10.22 Never use elastic bandages, paper towels, toilet tissue, or any other material that could shred and cling to the wound.

*Answer: True, Page: 173, Difficulty Level - E

10.23 A wet dressing is a dressing that is moist, but not necessarily sterile.

*Answer: True, Page: 173, Difficulty Level - M

10.24 Gauze pads are also referred to as multi-trauma dressings.

*Answer: False, Page: 174, Difficulty Level – M

10.25 The two most common mistakes in bandaging are bandaging too tightly and not covering the entire dressing.

*Answer: False, Page: 175, Difficulty Level - M

10.26 If a bandage becomes loose, wounds may bleed or become infected and broken bones can further displace.

*Answer: True, Page: 175, Difficulty Level - E

10.27 A bandage should never be placed directly against a wound.

*Answer: True, Page: 173, Difficulty Level - M

10.28 An elastic roller bandage should no be used except in cases of profuse bleeding, because it can create a tourniquet effect.

*Answer: True, Page: 176, Difficulty Level - E

10.29 Adaptability and creativity are more important than are the rules for bandaging.

*Answer: True, Page: 178, Difficulty Level - M

10.30 The tips of the fingers and toes should be covered when arms and legs are bandaged.

*Answer: False, Page: 178, Difficulty Level - M

10.31 Slings are used to support injuries of the shoulder, upper and lower extremities and the ribs.

*Answer: True, Page: 178, Difficulty Level - M

CHAPTER ELEVEN
MUSCULOSKELETAL INJURIES

MULTIPLE CHOICE

11.1 The human musculoskeletal system is composed of ______ bones, ______ types of joints and more than ______ muscles.

(A) 300, 10, 200
(B) 206, 8, 300
(C) 206, 6, 600
(D) 306, 16, 206

*Answer: C, Page: 187, Difficulty Level - M

11.2 Which of the following is one of the four major functions of the skeletal system?

(A) to give shape and form to the body
(B) to support the body
(C) to protect major body organs
(D) all of the above

*Answer: D, Page: 187, Difficulty Level - M

11.3 A special type of tissue that contracts when stimulated is:

(A) muscle
(B) tendon
(C) ligament
(D) joint

*Answer: A, Page: 187, Difficulty Level - E

11.4 Highly specialized connective tissue that attaches muscle to bone is:

(A) fibers
(B) tendons
(C) ligaments
(D) none of the above

*Answer: B, Page: 187, Difficulty Level - E

11.5 The ligament is often injured simultaneously with the:

(A) tendon
(B) muscle
(C) joint
(D) bone

*Answer: C, Page: 187, Difficulty Level - M

11.6 An injury in which ligaments are stretched and partially or completely torn is a:

(A) sprain
(B) strain
(C) dislocation
(D) none of the above

*Answer: A, Page: 187, Difficulty Level - M

11.7 When treating a sprain, the **"I"** in the acronym RICE stands for:

(A) immobilize
(B) isolate
(C) ice
(D) immediate

*Answer: C, Page: 188, Difficulty Level - E

11.8 Because dislocations are often accompanied by fractures, you should immobilize all dislocations.

(A) as straight as possible
(B) in the position found
(C) in its most natural position
(D) none of the above

*Answer: B, Page: 189, Difficulty Level - M

11.9 Bone or joint injuries can be one of two types:

(A) direct ro indirect
(B) simple or complex
(C) open or closed
(D) single or multiple

*Answer: C, Page: 190, Difficulty Level - C

11.10 When assessing bone injuries, you can get a good idea of how much additional damage may have occurred by determining:

(A) the amount of blood
(B) the amount of pain
(C) the mechanism of injury
(D) the position of the victim

*Answer: C, Page: 190, Difficulty Level - M

11.11 A women riding a horse, is thrown from the horse and lands on two outstretched hands. One arm sustains a fractured wrist and the collarbone at the end of the other arm is fractured. This is an example of what kind of force?

(A) direct
(B) indirect
(C) twisting
(D) none of the above

*Answer: B, Page: 191, Difficulty Level - M

11.12 What is the most important emergency care for suspected fracture or extensive soft-tissue injury?

(A) immobilization
(B) controlling pain
(C) controlling bleeding
(D) preventing shock

*Answer: A, Page: 193, Difficulty Level - M

11.13 Identifying signs and symptoms of bone and joint injury should be done ________ the primary survey.

(A) before
(B) after
(C) during

*Answer: B, Page: 192, Difficulty Level - E

11.14 Check the distal pulse of the suspected fracture site; if circulation is poor, immediately check for:

(A) internal bleeding
(B) pressure on a blood vessel
(C) additional fractures
(D) A or B

*Answer: D, Page: 193, Difficulty Level - M

11.15 Which of the following would be true when following general rules for applying a splint?

(A) splint an injury in the position you found it
(B) replace protruding bone ends
(C) apply pressure at the wound to control bleeding and swelling
(D) all of the above

*Answer: A, Page: 195, Difficulty Level - M

11.16 You should immobilize the joint ______ the fracture.

(A) above
(B) below
(C) above and below
(D) closest to

*Answer: C, Page: 195, Difficulty Level - M

11.17 In which of the following situations would you not splint a fracture?

(A) if it causes more pain for the victim
(B) if the wounded area is bleeding
(C) if the victim is unconscious
(D) if the victim is in shock

*Answer: A, Page: 195, Difficulty Level - M

11.18 Which of the following is not a function of a traction splint?

(A) to minimize further damage
(B) to alleviate pain
(C) to reduce fracture
(D) to reduce blood loss

*Answer: C, Page: 196, Difficulty Level - C

11.19 Which type of splint would be the most likely to impair circulation?

(A) rigid
(B) pneumatic
(C) traction
(D) improvised

*Answer: B, Page: 196, Difficulty Level - M

11.20 A splint that provides a counter-pull, alleviates pain and reduces blood loss is a:

(A) rigid splint
(B) traction splint
(C) pneumatic splint
(D) improvised splint

*Answer: B, Page: 196, Difficulty Level - M

11.21 An improvised splint should be:

(A) light in weight
(B) firm and rigid
(C) as wide as the thickest part of the fracture limb
(D) all of the above

*Answer: D, Page: 197, Difficulty Level - M

11.22 Before and after splinting, it is important to assess:

(A) breathing patterns
(B) blood loss
(C) pulse
(D) consciousness

*Answer: C, Page: 199, Difficulty Level - M

11.23 Which of the following might result form improper splinting?

(A) compressed nerves, tissue and blood vessels
(B) reduced distal circulation
(C) aggravated bone or joint injury
(D) all of the above

*Answer: D, Page: 197, Difficulty Level - M

11.24 A soft-tissue injury or a muscle spasm around a joint is a:

(A) cramp
(B) sprain
(C) strain
(D) dislocation

*Answer: C, Page: 187, Difficulty Level - M

11.25 An improvised splint should be:

(A) light in weight
(B) firm and rigid
(C) as wide as the thickest part of the fracture
(D) all of the above

*Answer: D, Page: 189, Difficulty Level – M

TRUE / FALSE

11.26 In most cases you should care for a sprain as if it were a fracture, and immobilize it accordingly.

*Answer: True, Page: 187, Difficulty Level - M

11.27 A dislocation is a soft-tissue injury or a muscle spasm around a joint.

*Answer: False, Page: 189, Difficulty Level - E

11.28 If there is enough force to damage the pelvis or to cause severe head or facial injuries, you should also assume there are injuries to the spine.

*Answer: True, Page: 193, Difficulty Level - M

11.29 If you're not sure whether you should splint an injury or not, it's always safer not to splint.

*Answer: False, Page: 195, Difficulty Level - M

11.30 If the victim shows signs of shock, arrange for immediate transport without taking time to apply a splint.

*Answer: True, Page: 195, Difficulty Level - M

11.31 Improper splinting can actually make an injury worse.

*Answer: True, Page: 197, Difficulty Level - E

11.32 Paresthesia is a pricking or tingling sensation that indicates loss of circulation.

*Answer: True, Page: 197, Difficulty Level - M

11.33 In caring for sprains, the **"I"** in RICE stands for "immobilize".

*Answer: False, Page: 188, Difficulty Level – E

CHAPTER TWELVE
COMMON SPORT AND RECREATIONAL INJURIES

MULTIPLE CHOICE

12.1 In caring for a fractured clavicle, which of the following methods of splinting should you use?

(A) sling and swathe
(B) figure-eight bandage
(C) butterfly sling
(D) any of the above

*Answer: D, Page: 207, Difficulty Level - M

12.2 An obvious and palpable lump over the tip of the shoulder would be an indication of shoulder:

(A) separation
(B) dislocation
(C) fracture
(D) none of the above

*Answer: A, Page: 207, Difficulty Level - M

12.3 What type of splint should you avoid using on a dislocated elbow?

(A) ladder
(B) sam
(C) vacuum
(D) air

*Answer: D, Page: 210, Difficulty Level - M

12.4 The most common symptom of radial head fracture is:

(A) deformity
(B) pain while rotating the forearm
(C) shortened forearm on the injured side
(D) a golf-ball size lump on the back of the elbow

*Answer: B, Page: 210, Difficulty Level - C

12.5 In what position should you splint a dislocated elbow?

(A) flexed
(B) at a ninety degree angle
(C) in the position found
(D) none of the above

*Answer: C, Page: 210, Difficulty Level - M

12.6 How do Colles's and Smith's fractures differ from each other?

(A) in severity
(B) in their sings and symptoms
(C) in mechanism of injury
(D) all of the above

*Answer: C, Page: 210, Difficulty Level

12.7 The fracture that occurs from a victim falling on the palm of the hand with the wrist extended is a:

(A) Smith's fracture
(B) Colles's fracture
(C) radial head fracture
(D) dislocated wrist

*Answer: B, Page: 210, Difficulty Level - M

12.8 A classic sign of a Smith's fracture is:

(A) "silver fork deformity"
(B) a shortened forearm on the injured side
(C) inability to bend the elbow
(D) all of the above

*Answer: A, Page: 211, Difficulty Level - M

12.9 Colles's fractures are most common in:

(A) athletes
(B) elderly people
(C) children
(D) gymnasts

*Answer: C, Page: 210, Difficulty Level - M

12.10 When giving first-aid for a carpal fracture with no deformity use ________ splint.

(A) an air
(B) a ladder
(C) a vacuum
(D) a Sam

*Answer: A, Page: 211, Difficulty Level - M

12.11 In caring for metacarpal fractures, assess for circulation every few minutes by checking:

(A) for sensation in the finger tips
(B) for discoloration of the finger tips
(C) radial pulse
(D) capillary refill

*Answer: D, Page: 212, Difficulty Level - C

12.12 With non-displaced fractures of the fingers, there is usually a great deal of:

(A) swelling
(B) deformity
(C) pain
(D) all of the above

*Answer: C, Page: 212, Difficulty Level M

12.13 A tenderness when palpitating the anatomical snuff box is highly suggestive of a:

(A) Colles's fracture
(B) radial head fracture
(C) metacarpal fracture
(D) navicular fracture

*Answer: D, Page: 211, Difficulty Level - C

12.14 Signs and symptoms including limping, tenderness to the touch and red discoloration, later turning purple are indicative of:

(A) a hip pointer
(B) an ischial tuberosity fracture
(C) a hamstring strain
(D) none of the above

*Answer: A, Page: 213, Difficulty Level - M

12.15 If the victim is suffering from an ischial tuberosity fracture, he/she will feel pain in the:

(A) hip
(B) buttocks
(C) ankle
(D) knee

*Answer: B, Page: 213, Difficulty Level - M

12.16 When splinting a sprained knee, you should wrap the knee in a pillow splint:

(A) in the position found
(B) in a bent position
(C) in the most comfortable position
(D) as straight as possible

*Answer: C, Page: 214, Difficulty Level - C

12.17 Generally injuries that produce an audible "pop" are associated with the:

(A) hip
(B) elbow
(C) knee
(D) shoulder

*Answer: C, Page: 214, Difficulty Level - M

12.18 Unlike the ischial tuberosity fracture, hamstring strain occurs:

(A) mostly among the young
(B) mostly among the elderly
(C) among people who are out of shape
(D) among people of all ages

*Answer: D, Page: 213, Difficulty Level - M

12.19 Most frequently achilles tendon rupture results from:

(A) jumping and cutting maneuvers
(B) blunt trauma
(C) a direct fall
(D) hyperextension

*Answer: A, Page: 215, Difficulty Level - M

TRUE / FALSE

12.20 The acromioclavicular joint is the joint in the shoulder where the clavicle and scapula join.

*Answer: True, Page: 207, Difficulty Level - M

12.21 A shoulder separation is more severe an injury than a dislocation.

*Answer: False, Page: 208, Difficulty Level - M

12.22 To care for a mild shoulder separation, immobilize the shoulder with a roller or elastic bandage.

*Answer: True, Page: 208, Difficulty Level - M

12.23 Because the growth plate just above the wrist does not fully mature until around the age of eighteen, children and adolescents are more prone to fracture.

*Answer: True, Page: 210, Difficulty Level - M

12.24 The most commonly fractured carpal bone is the navicular which has a limited blood supply and heals very poorly unless promptly and properly treated.

*Answer: True, Page: 211, Difficulty Level - C

12.25 Applying a sling and swathe or an elastic bandage is appropriate when caring for a dislocated shoulder.

*Answer: False, Page: 216, Difficulty Level - M

12.26 Because it can be difficult to distinguish between fractures and other injuries, generally, victims of sports injuries should be evaluated by a physician.

*Answer: True, Page: 216, Difficulty Level – E

11.27 The fingers are the most commonly broken bones in the body.

*Answer: True, Page: 212, Difficulty Level - E

CHAPTER THIRTEEN
HEAD AND SPINE INJURIES

MULTIPLE CHOICE

13.1 Fifty percent of head injuries are caused by:

(A) assaults and violence
(B) falls
(C) motor vehicle crashes
(D) sports and recreation

*Answer: C, Page: 221, Difficulty Level - M

13.2 A brain injury in which the head comes to a sudden stop but the brain continues to move back and forth inside the skull is:

(A) coup-contrecoup
(B) a brain contusion
(C) an epidermal hematoma
(D) a subdural hematoma

*Answer: A, Page: 222, Difficulty Level - M

13.3 Bleeding between the skull and protective covering of the brain is:

(A) a brain contusion
(B) a subdural hematoma
(C) an epidural hematoma
(D) none of the above

*Answer: C, Page: 222, Difficulty Level - M

13.4 The most common type of skull fracture that causes a thin-line crack in the skull is a:

(A) linear fracture
(B) basal fracture
(C) comminuted fracture
(D) depressed fracture

*Answer: A, Page: 223, Difficulty Level - E

13.5 A fracture that occurs when there is a break in the bed of the skull, is difficult to detect and often causes extensive damage is a:

(A) depressed fracture
(B) linear fracture
(C) comminuted fracture
(D) basal fracture

*Answer: D, Page: 223, Difficulty Level - M

13.6 When assessing a victim of head injury, it is important to obtain a history that includes:

(A) whether the victim's level of consciousness has changed
(B) whether the victim has been moved
(C) the mechanism of injury
(D) all of the above

*Answer: D, Page: 225, Difficulty Level - M

13.7 The most serious complication of a head injury is:

(A) extensive bleeding
(B) shock
(C) lack of oxygen to the brain
(D) impaired ventilation

*Answer: C, Page: 225, Difficulty Level - M

13.8 One of the signs of skull fracture is Battle's sign which is:

(A) bruising around the eyes
(B) bruising behind the ears
(C) fluid leaking from the ears, nose or mouth
(D) deformity of the skull

*Answer: B, Page: 226, Difficulty Level - M

13.9 Before beginning any emergency care for head injury, first:

(A) immobilize the victim
(B) assess level of consciousness
(C) control bleeding
(D) remove any penetrating objects

*Answer: B, Page: 227, Difficulty Level - M

13.10 Whenever you care for a victim of head injury, always assume:

(A) skull fracture
(B) brain damage
(C) spinal injury
(D) all of the above

*Answer: D, Page: 227-228, Difficulty Level - M

13.11 After activating the EMS system, the top priority of emergency care for a head injury is to:

(A) control bleeding
(B) immobilize the victim
(C) establish and maintain an open airway
(D) treat for shock

*Answer: C, Page: 228, Difficulty Level - M

13.12 If the victim sustained a medical or non-traumatic injury, place the victim on his or her:

(A) back
(B) right side
(C) left side
(D) stomach

*Answer: C, Page: 229, Difficulty Level - M

13.13 The largest number of spinal cord injuries are caused by:

(A) shallow-water swimming/diving accidents
(B) car accidents
(C) motorcycle accidents
(D) sledding accidents

*Answer: B, Page: 229, Difficulty level - M

13.14 The sudden pulling apart of the spine that stretches and tears the cord is:

(A) lateral bending
(B) excessive flexion
(C) compression
(D) distraction

*Answer: D, Page: 229, Difficulty Level - M

13.15 In which of the following situations should you always suspect spinal injury?

(A) unwitnessed near-drownings
(B) hangings
(C) motorcycle accidents
(D) all of the above

*Answer: D, Page: 231, Difficulty Level - M

13.16 The two major complications of spinal injury are inadequate breathing effort and:

(A) paralysis
(B) unconsciousness
(C) bleeding
(D) impaired circulation

*Answer: A, Page: 231, Difficulty Level - M

13.17 Half of all spinal injuries occur in the ________ spinal region.

(A) sacral
(B) lumbar
(C) thoracic
(D) cervical

*Answer: D, Page: 229, Difficulty Level - M

13.18 The first step in assessing a responsive victim of spinal injury is to:

(A) assess equality of strength
(B) note the mechanism of injury
(C) inspect for deformities and swelling
(D) ask, "Can you feel me touching your toes"?

*Answer: B, Page: 232, Difficulty Level - M

13.19 Pain associated with movement is a sign of spinal injury. Assess the victim's pain by:

(A) asking the victim to move
(B) moving the victim yourself
(C) basing your assessment on any movement that occurred before you arrived on the scene
(D) obvious deformity

*Answer: C, Page: 232, Difficulty Level - M

13.20 What is the most reliable sign of spinal injury?

(A) impaired breathing
(B) paralysis in the extremities
(C) pain associated with movement
(D) obvious deformity

*Answer: B, Page: 234, Difficulty Level - M

13.21 What technique should you use to open the airway of a victim with spinal injury?

(A) modified jaw-thrust
(B) head-tilt / chin-lift
(C) chin-lift only
(D) none of the above

*Answer: A, Page: 235, Difficulty Level - M

13.22 When performing emergency care for spinal injuries, which of the following is not true?

(A) never try to stop the flow of blood or fluid from ears, nose or mouth
(B) never perform CPR
(C) never apply pressure to a bleeding head wound if you suspect fracture
(D) never move the victim

*Answer: B, Page: 236, Difficulty Level - M

13.23 Under which of the following circumstances should you remove the helmet of a spinal-injured victim?

(A) if the helmet interferes with your ability to assess breathing
(B) if the helmet interferes with proper spinal immobilization
(C) if the victim is in cardiac arrest
(D) all of the above

*Answer: D, Page: 236, Difficulty Level - M

13.24 The general rule for management of spinal injury is to support and immobilize the:

(A) spine
(B) head
(C) torso and pelvis
(D) all of the above

*Answer: D, Page: 235, Difficulty Level - M

TRUE / FALSE

13.25 While head injury constitutes only a small percentage of all injures, it causes more than half of all fatalities from injuries.

*Answer: True, Page: 220, Difficulty Level - M

13.26 Skull fracture itself presents no danger unless accompanied by brain injury.

*Answer: True, Page: 223, Difficulty Level - M

13.27 When assessing a head wound, palpitate the wound to determine size and depth of the injury.

*Answer: False, Page: 225, Difficulty Level - M

13.28 To control bleeding of an open or depressed skull injury, apply direct pressure.

*Answer: False, Page: 228, Difficulty Level - E

13.29 The extent of assessment of a spinal injured victim should be based on the level of training the first aider has had under the direction of a qualified and certified instructor.

*Answer: True, Page: 232, Difficulty Level - M

13.30 You can generally rule-out the possibility of spinal column or spinal cord damage if the victim can walk or move his or her arms and legs.

*Answer: False, Page: 232, Difficulty Level - M

13.31 A fracture of one spot on the spine is usually associated with a fracture in other areas of the spine.

*Answer: True, Page: 232, Difficulty Level - M

CHAPTER FOURTEEN
POISONING EMERGENCIES

MULTIPLE CHOICE

14.1 Poisoning is the __________ cause of accidental death among children.

(A) number one
(B) second leading
(C) third leading
(D) fourth leading

*Answer: A, Page: 242, Difficulty Level - M

14.2 Which of the following questions should you ask the victim or bystanders when taking a history from a poisoning victim?

(A) What was ingested?
(B) When was the substance taken?
(C) How much was taken?
(D) all of the above

*Answer: D, Page: 244, Difficulty Level - E

14.3 To manage a poisoning victim correctly, it is important to get:

(A) consent
(B) the victim's vital signs
(C) a relevant history
(D) none of the above

*Answer: C, Page: 244, Difficulty Level - M

14.4 Noxious dusts, gases and fumes are poisons that enter the body through:

(A) ingestion
(B) inhalation
(C) injection
(D) absorption

*Answer: B, Page: 242, Difficulty Level - E

14.5 How many of all poisoning incidents involve drugs?

(A) one-fourth
(B) two-thirds
(C) one-half
(D) three-fourths

*Answer: B, Page: 242, Difficulty Level - C

14.6 What is the number one cause of accidental death among children?

(A) drowning
(B) burns/fire
(C) poisoning
(D) none of the above

*Answer: C, Page: 242, Difficulty Level - E

14.7 Which of the following might suggest poisoning by ingestion?

(A) abdominal pain
(B) unusual breath or body odors
(C) excessive salivation
(D) all of the above

*Answer: D, Page: 244, Difficulty Level - M

14.8 The incidence of food poisoning is __________ each year.

(A) decreasing
(B) increasing slightly
(C) remaining the same
(D) increasing dramatically

*Answer: D, Page: 245, Difficulty Level - M

14.9 After activating the EMS system, the next step in providing emergency care to a poisoned victim is to:

(A) contact poison control
(B) check for any resulting injuries
(C) maintain the airway
(D) induce vomiting

*Answer: C, Page: 244, Difficulty Level - M

14.10 In most cases, poison control professionals will instruct you to:

(A) have the victim drink water to dilute the agent
(B) induce vomiting before the substance enters the intestinal tract
(C) administer activated charcoal to absorb the poison
(D) none of the above

*Answer: C, Page: 244, Difficulty Level - M

14.11 Most toxic inhalation occurs as a result of:

(A) fumes from liquid chemicals
(B) fires
(C) sewer gas
(D) incomplete combustion of natural gas

*Answer: B, Page: 247, Difficulty Level – M

14.12 Which of the following is <u>not</u> true concerning carbon monoxide poisoning?

(A) it is completely tasteless, colorless and odorless
(B) it causes twenty-five percent of all poisoning deaths in the U.S. each year
(C) it reduces the amount of oxygen carried by the bloodstream
(D) it takes only a few minutes to die from carbon monoxide poisoning

*Answer: B, Page: 247, Difficulty Level - C

14.13 The initial signs and symptoms of carbon monoxide poisoning are similar to those of:

(A) the flu
(B) poisoning by ingestion
(C) respiratory distress
(D) food poisoning

*Answer: A, Page: 248, Difficulty Level - M

14.14 Which of the following is a sign or symptom of a high level of carbon monoxide?

(A) chest pain
(B) temporary loss of vision
(C) lethargy and stupor
(D) all of the above

*Answer: D, Page: 248, Difficulty Level - M

14.15 After activating the EMS system, the next priority when caring for a victim of inhaled poisons is to:

(A) get the victim into fresh air
(B) check for contraindicating injuries
(C) start artificial ventilation
(D) none of the above

*Answer: A, Page: 248, Difficulty Level – M

14.16 If you suspect the victim has inhaled carbon monoxide, move the victim at least ________ feet from the suspected source of the carbon monoxide.

(A) 50
(B) 100
(C) 150
(D) 200

*Answer: C, Page: 248, Difficulty Level - C

14.17 What position is best for a victim of inhaled poison if there are no contraindicating injuries?

(A) sitting-up
(B) standing
(C) lying down with head elevated
(D) lying down with feet elevated

*Answer: C, Page: 248-249, Difficulty Level - M

14.18 Illicit drugs can be injected:

(A) under the skin
(B) into the muscle
(C) into the bloodstream
(D) all of the above

*Answer: D, Page: 249, Difficulty Level - E

14.19 Injected poisons usually cause _________ reaction at the injection site:

(A) a delayed
(B) no
(C) an immediate
(D) an allergic

*Answer: C, Page: 249, Difficulty Level – M

14.20 When providing emergency care for a victim of injected poison, after activating the EMS system, you should next:

(A) protect yourself and the victim
(B) maintain the victim's airway
(C) be alert for vomiting
(D) identify the source of the injury

*Answer: B, Page: 249, Difficulty Level - M

14.21 Which of the following is a sign or symptom of absorbed poisons?

(A) vomiting
(B) abdominal pain
(C) altered mental status
(D) itching or irritation

*Answer: D, Page: 251, Difficulty Level - M

14.22 The greatest danger from injected poison is:

(A) vomiting
(B) a change in heart rate
(C) loss of consciousness
(D) anaphylactic shock

*Answer: D, Page: 249, Difficulty Level - M

14.23 activated charcoal should be used for victims who have _______ poison.

(A) ingested
(B) absorbed
(C) injected
(D) inhaled

*Answer: A, Page: 246, Difficulty Level – E

14.24 Under which of the following circumstance should you <u>not</u> give activated charcoal to a victim?

(A) if the victim is not fully conscious
(B) if the victim has swallowed acids or alkalies
(C) if the victim is unable to swallow
(D) all of the above

*Answer: D, Page: 246, Difficulty Level - M

14.25 Activated charcoal works by ________ contaminants.

(A) neutralizing
(B) dissolving
(C) absorbing
(D) activating

*Answer: C, Page: 246, Difficulty Level - M

14.26 Do not give activated charcoal to a victim who has ingested:

(A) alcohol
(B) acids
(C) aspirin
(D) A & B

*Answer: D, Page: 246, Difficulty Level - M

TRUE / FALSE

14.27 Management of ingestion poisoning is aimed at ridding the body of poison before it enters the intestinal tract.

*Answer: True, Page: 243, Difficulty Level - M

14.28 Half of all plant poisonings are caused by mushrooms.

*Answer: True, Page: 243, Difficulty Level - M

14.29 If all signs and symptoms of a poisoned victim have been controlled, the victim generally does not need to see a physician.

*Answer: False, Page: 245, Difficulty Level – E

14.30 Food poisoning is difficult to detect because the signs and symptoms vary greatly.

*Answer: True, Page: 245, Difficulty Level - M

14.31 If you suspect food poisoning, give the victim milk or ice cream to neutralize the poison.

*Answer: False, Page:245, Difficulty Level - M

14.32 The body absorbs inhaled poisons very rapidly, so immediate care is critical.

*Answer: True, Page: 247, Difficulty Level - M

14.33 The signs and symptoms of carbon monoxide change with time and intensity of poisoning.

*Answer: True, Page: 248, Difficulty Level - M

14.34 If people and pets in the same environment share the same symptoms, you should suspect carbon monoxide poisoning.

*Answer: True, Page: 248, Difficulty Level - M

14.35 It is best to use activated charcoal in the powder form because it stays active longer than the pre-mixed.

*Answer: False, Page: 246, Difficulty Level - M

14.36 The more skin affected by as absorbed poison, the greater the need for medical attention.

*Answer: True, Page: 251, Difficulty Level - E

CHAPTER FIFTEEN
DRUG AND ALCOHOL EMERGENCIES

MULTIPLE CHOICE

15.1 What is the most abused drug in the United States?

(A) PCP
(B) alcohol
(C) cocaine
(D) over the counter drugs

*Answer: B, Page: 256, Difficulty Level - M

15.2 Which of the following would you do if you suspect an unconscious victim might be experiencing a drug or alcohol emergency?

(A) inspect the area for evidence
(B) check the victim's mouth for signs of partially dissolved pills
(C) smell the victim's breath for traces of alcohol
(D) all of the above

*Answer: D, Page: 258, Difficulty Level - M

15.3 Which of the following signs and symptoms of a drug or alcohol related emergency would indicate a life-threatening emergency?

(A) a fever over 100 degrees
(B) vomiting while not fully conscious
(C) breathing difficulties
(D) all of the above

*Answer: D, Page: 258, Difficulty Level - M

15.4 An abnormal or irregular pulse lower than ________ beats per minute would indicate a life-threatening emergency.

(A) 60
(B) 70
(C) 80
(D) none of the above

*Answer: A, Page: 258, Difficulty Level - M

15.5 Alcohol is completely absorbed from the stomach and intestinal tract within:

(A) two hours
(B) three hours
(C) four hours
(D) one hour

*Answer: A, Page: 258, Difficulty Level - C

15.6 There are four general stages of alcohol withdrawal. Major seizures occurring within 48 hours characterize which stage?

(A) stage one
(B) stage two
(C) stage three
(D) stage four

*Answer: C, Page: 260, Difficulty Level - C

15.7 Which of the following signs and symptoms characterize stage two of withdrawal syndrome?

(A) insomnia, sweating nausea
(B) major seizures
(C) delirium tremens
(D) vomiting, illusion or hallucinations

*Answer: D, Page: 260, Difficulty Level - M

15.8 Which of the following is <u>not</u> a sign or symptom of delirium tremens?

(A) loss of memory
(B) seizures
(C) nausea
(D) dilated pupils

*Answer: B, Page: 262, Difficulty Level - C

15.9 A victim who responds appropriately to verbal or noxious stimuli but will fall asleep when the stimuli is removed, falls into which category of level of consciousness?

(A) awake
(B) semicomatose
(C) comatose

*Answer: B, Page: 262, Difficulty Level - M

15.10 When obtaining a history of a victim of a drug/alcohol-related emergency, which of the following information is the <u>least</u> important?

(A) what was taken
(B) when was it taken
(C) age and weight of the victim
(D) how much was taken

*Answer: C, Page: 263, Difficulty Level - M

15.11 Which of the following is a sign that immediate medical attention is needed?

(A) disturbances of vision
(B) grand mal seizures
(C) nervous system depression
(D) all of the above

*Answer: D, Page: 263, Difficulty Level - M

15.12 Which of the following is not a goal of crisis intervention when managing a drug/alcohol crisis?

(A) to create trust
(B) to lower anxiety
(C) to provide counseling
(D) to establish rapport

*Answer: C, Page: 263, Difficulty Level - M

15.13 Which of the following is not one of the general guidelines for managing a drug/alcohol crisis?

(A) establish a relationship
(B) provide a reality base
(C) encourage communication
(D) foster confidence

*Answer: A, Page: 263, Difficulty Level - C

15.14 The primary concern in acute intoxication is:

(A) maintaining an airway
(B) preventing further injury
(C) maintaining consciousness
(D) activating the EMS system

*Answer: A, Page: 264, Difficulty Level - M

15.15 The dangers associated with marijuana are primarily _______ in nature.

(A) physical
(B) psychological
(C) emotional
(D) none of the above

*Answer: B, Page: 265, Difficulty Level - E

15.16 What is the preferred method for handling "bad trips"?

(A) isolation
(B) restraint
(C) the talk-down technique
(D) professional counseling

*Answer: C, Page: 265, Difficulty Level - M

15.17 Which of the following would be part of providing appropriate non-verbal support when managing a drug/alcohol crisis?

(A) using the victim's name
(B) asking clear, simple questions
(C) maintaining eye contact
(D) responding to feelings

*Answer: C, Page: 263, Difficulty Level - E

15.18 Which of the following would be important when handling a victim of overdose?

(A) maintaining proper body temperature
(B) establishing a clear airway
(C) reducing stimuli
(D) all of the above

*Answer: D, Page: 265, Difficulty Level - M

15.19 You should not use __________ when handling a victim who has used PCP.

(A) the talk-down technique
(B) artificial ventilation
(C) direct eye contact
(D) physical restraint

*Answer: A, Page: 265, Difficulty Level - M

15.20 Which of the following is <u>not</u> true about the drug PCP?

(A) it is known by at least fort-six names
(B) it is cheap, easy to make, east to take
(C) it is known as the "equal opportunity" drug
(D) it is related to horrible psychological effects

*Answer: C, Page: 267, Difficulty Level - C

15.21 Which of the following might be a reaction stemming from high doses of PCP?

(A) schizophrenia
(B) paranoia
(C) memory loss
(D) all of the above

*Answer: D, Page: 267, Difficulty Level - M

15.22 Which of the following is the drug most often involved in emergency room visits?

(A) PCP
(B) cocaine
(C) aspirin
(D) none of the above

*Answer: B, Page: 267, Difficulty Level - M

15.23 When handling victims of cocaine intoxication, always take extra measures to protect yourself from:

(A) AIDS and other infectious diseases
(B) legal liability
(C) violent outbursts
(D) concealed weapons

*Answer: A, Page: 267, Difficulty Level - M

15.24 Which of the following might be an indication that a violent drug victim is about to lose control?

(A) eyes fixated open with a blank stare
(B) unresponsiveness to pain
(C) excessive sweating and agitation
(D) all of the above

*Answer: C, Page: 268, Difficulty Level - C

15.25 Because PCP is ________ the victim will probably be unaware of ________.

(A) an anesthetic, pain
(B) a depressant, immediate surroundings
(C) a stimulant, time
(D) a depressant, familiar faces

*Answer: A, Page: 267, Difficulty Level - M

TRUE / FALSE

15.26 Drug abusers are more prone to certain injuries, illnesses and infectious diseases.

*Answer: True, Page: 256, Difficulty Level - M

15.27 It is difficult to assess drug or alcohol emergencies properly because drugs and alcohol produce signs that mimic a number of system disorders and diseases.

*Answer: True, Page: 258, Difficulty Level - M

15.28 You can safely assume that if a person is stuporous or has slurred speech, he or she is a victim of drug overdose.

*Answer: False, Page: 258, Difficulty Level - M

15.29 Acute intoxication often mimics insulin shock so you should always suspect diabetes and give the victim sugar if in doubt.

*Answer: True, Page: 259, Difficulty Level - M

15.30 Withdrawal syndrome is dose dependent; the more the alcoholic was drinking, the more severe the syndrome will be.

*Answer: True, Page: 260, Difficulty Level - M

15.31 A single episode of DT's lasts between one and three hours; multiple episodes can last as long as a week.

*Answer: False, Page: 262, Difficulty Level - C

15.32 If a victim of drug overdose seems to be hyperventilating, have the victim breathe into a paper bag.

*Answer: False, Page: 264, Difficulty Level - M

15.33 For your own safety and the safety of the victim, as a general rule, you should automatically restrain a victim of drug overdose.

*Answer: False, Page: 265, Difficulty Level - M

15.34 If a user of PCP suddenly loses weight, the drug can be released into the bloodstream even if the drug has not been recently taken.

*Answer: True, Page: 266, Difficulty Level - M

CHAPTER SIXTEEN
POISONING EMERGENCIES

MULTIPLE CHOICE

16.1 A condition in which fatty substances and other debris are deposited on the arterial walls is:

(A) arteriosclerosis
(B) atherosclerosis
(C) myocardial infarction
(D) angina pectoris

*Answer: B, Page: 273, Difficulty Level - M

16.2 Arteriosclerosis can lead to:

(A) hypertension
(B) kidney disease
(C) stroke
(D) all of the above

*Answer: D, Page: 274, Difficulty Level - M

16.3 Which of the following factors increase the likelihood of myocardial infarction?

(A) diabetes
(B) age
(C) smoking
(D) all of the above

*Answer: D, Page: 274, Difficulty Level - E

16.4 The risk for a victim with high cholesterol levels, high blood pressure, and heavy smoking is____________times that of someone without those risk factors.

(A) ten times
(B) five times
(C) twenty times
(D) fifteen times

*Answer: A, Page: 274, Difficulty Level - C

16.5 Arteriosclerosis occurs when arteries lose their:

(A) shape
(B) size
(C) elasticity
(D) none of the above

*Answer: C, Page: 274, Difficulty Level - E

16.6 Angina pectoris literally means:

(A) hardening of the arteries
(B) pain in the chest
(C) coronary artery disease
(D) heart attack

*Answer: B, Page: 275, Difficulty Level - M

16.7 Angina occurs when the hearts' demand for____________ is greater than what it is receiving.

(A) blood
(B) oxygen
(C) nutrients
(D) stimulus

*Answer: B, Page: 275, Difficulty Level -M

16.8 Which of the following is true about angina pectoris?

(A) angina is irreversible
(B) angina is reversible
(C) angina produces permanent damage to the heart
(D) angina can be fatal

*Answer: B, Page: 275, Difficulty Level - M

16.9 The most common sign of angina is:

(A) palpitations
(B) nausea and/or vomiting
(C) dyspnea
(D) chest pain

*Answer: D, Page: 275, Difficulty Level - M

16.10 Angina usually appears suddenly and is associated with:

(A) improper nutrition
(B) smoking /lung disease
(C) physical exertion
(D) respiratory complications

*Answer: C, Page: 275, Difficulty Level - M

16.11 The most dramatic sign of congestive heart failure is:

(A) anxiety
(B) rapid heart rate
(C) paleness or cyanosis
(D) pulmonary edema

*Answer: D, Page: 276, Difficulty Level - M

16.12 Which of the following conditions is likely to produce chest pain?

(A) respiratory infection
(B) over exertion
(C) indigestion
(D) all of the above

*Answer: D, Page: 275, Difficulty Level - M

16.13 A condition in which plasma seeps out of the capillaries into the lungs due to pressure from a failing heart is:

(A) pulmonary edema
(B) myocardial infarction
(C) congestive heart failure
(D) coronary artery disease

*Answer: A, Page: 277, Difficulty Level - M

16.14 When the blood supply to the heart is restricted or cut off, the result is:

(A) pulmonary edema
(B) congestive heart failure
(C) angina pectoris
(D) myocardial infarction

*Answer: D, Page: 277, Difficulty Level - M

16.15 Which of the following is true concerning a thrombus stroke?

(A) most occur in people over the age of 50
(B) the incidence increases with age
(C) clots form around damaged artery walls
(D) all of the above

*Answer: D, Page: 282, Difficulty Level - M

16.16 The characteristics of a stroke depend on:

(A) the extent of the stroke
(B) the site of the stroke
(C) the amount of brain damage that results
(D) all of the above

*Answer: D. Page: 281, Difficulty Level - C

16.17 Approximately 75 to 85 percent of all strokes are caused by:

(A) embolus
(B) hemorrhage
(C) thrombus
(D) compression

*Answer: C, Page: 282, Difficulty Level - M

16.18 A transient ischemic attack is:

(A) a "mini" heart attack
(B) similar to a stroke
(C) a shortness of breath
(D) none of the above

*Answer: B, Page: 282, Difficulty Level - M

16.19 Which of the following is <u>not</u> associated with TIA's?

(A) blindness in one eye
(B) temporary paralysis of the face
(C) light-headedness
(D) nausea or vomiting

*Answer: D, Page: 283, Difficulty Level - C

16.20 Which of the following statements about cerebral embolisms is true?

(A) Of all strokes, cerebral embolisms have the most rapid onset.
(B) Cerebral embolisms often occur in young or middle-aged adults.
(C) Cerebral embolism are most common among people with existing heart disease.
(D) all of the above

*Answer: D, Page: 283, Difficulty Level - M

16.21 Because of its dramatic nature, 80 percent of the victims of this form of stroke die.

(A) thrombus
(B) hemorrhage
(C) embolus
(D) compression

*Answer: B, Page: 283, Difficulty Level - M

16.22 A stroke that produces a sudden excruciating headache followed by a rapid loss of consciousness, neck rigidity, and coma is caused by:

(A) embolus
(B) compression
(C) cerebral hemorrhage
(D) thrombus

*Answer: C, Page: 283, Difficulty Level - M

16.23 You should position the conscious victim of a stroke:

(A) on his back with head and shoulders slightly raised
(B) on his back with head turned to one side
(C) on his side, paralyzed side up
(D) on his back with feet raised

*Answer: A, Page: 284, Difficulty Level - M

16.24 To treat a responsive cardiac victim, activate the EMS system, then:

(A) give the victim nitroglycerin
(B) loosen restrictive clothing
(C) perform an initial assessment
(D) keep the victim warm

*Answer: C, Page: 280, Difficulty Level - C

16.25 If allowed to in your area, under which of the following circumstances should you help a victim take nitroglycerin?

(A) if the systolic blood pressure is below 100 mmHg
(B) if the systolic blood pressure is above 100 mmHg
(C) if the victim is an infant or child
(D) if the victim has already taken the maximum dose, but is still feeling discomfort

*Answer: B, Page: 281, Difficulty Level - M

16.26 Generally, the best way to relieve angina pectoris is to:

(A) rest
(B) take nitroglycerin
(C) exercise
(D) control your diet

*Answer: A, Page: 285 (summary), Difficulty Level - M

TRUE / FALSE

16.27 Heart attacks and associated heart disease are the number-one killer in the United States today.

*Answer: True, Page: 272, Difficulty Level - M

16.28 Because of the critical nature of heart disease emergencies, you should treat every adult with chest pain as a heart attack victim until proven otherwise.

*Answer: True, Page: 272, Difficulty Level - M

16.29 Atherosclerosis is a disease condition in which the arteries lose their elasticity.

*Answer: False, Page: 273, Difficulty Level - M

16.30 It is impossible for a First Aider to tell the difference between the pain of angina pectoris and the pain of a heart attack.

*Answer: True, Page: 275, Difficulty Level - M

16.31 Generally, congestive heart failure is both treatable and curable.

*Answer: False, Page: 276, Difficulty Level - M

16.32 Twenty-five percent of all myocardial infarctions victims have no chest pain at all.

*Answer: True, Page: 277, Difficulty Level - M

16.33 It is crucial to determine at the scene the kind of stroke that occurred, because emergency care will differ according to the cause of the stroke.

*Answer: False, Page: 284, Difficulty Level - C

16.34 If the victim of a stroke develops difficulty breathing or becomes unconscious, turn him on his side with the paralyzed side up.

*Answer: False, Page: 285, Difficulty Level - C

16.35 You should not allow a victim to take nitroglycerin if you suspect the victim has a head injury.

*Answer: True, Page: 281, Difficulty Level - M

CHAPTER SEVENTEEN
RESPIRATORY EMERGENCIES

MULTIPLE CHOICE

17.1 A sensation of shortness of breath - a feeling of air hunger accompanied by labored breathing, defines:

(A) asthma
(B) dyspnea
(C) respiratory distress
(D) none of the above

*Answer: B, Page: 291, Difficulty Level - M

17.2 Which of the following would most likely cause true dyspnea?

(A) exercise
(B) coughing
(C) aspiration of a foreign body
(D) all of the above

*Answer: C, Page: 291, Difficulty Level - M

17.3 Which one of the following emergency care procedures would you apply for a victim with dyspnea after checking for aspiration and clearing the airway?

(A) treat for shock
(B) control bleeding
(C) CPR
(D) artificial ventilation

*Answer: A, Page: 291, Difficulty Level - M

17.4 Dyspnea is generally characterized by ________ and ________ breathing.

(A) deep, labored
(B) rapid, shallow
(C) slow, deep
(D) slow, labored

*Answer: B, Page: 291, Difficulty Level - C

17.5 A respiratory disease characterized by overinflated alveoli is:

(A) asthma
(B) chronic bronchitis
(C) dyspnea
(D) emphysema

*Answer: D, Page: 291, Difficulty Level - M

17.6 Which of the following is a sign or symptom of emphysema?

(A) barrel-shaped chest
(B) lungs remain expanded even after exhalation
(C) evidence of weight loss
(D) all of the above

*Answer: D, Page: 291, Difficulty Level - M

17.7 "Pink puffers" refers to victims of:

(A) emphysema
(B) chronic bronchitis
(C) asthma
(D) all of the above

*Answer: A, Page: 291, Difficulty Level - M

17.8 A productive cough that has persisted for at least three months out of the year over the past two consecutive years would indicate:

(A) emphysema
(B) chronic bronchitis
(C) asthma
(D) none of the above

*Answer: B, Page: 292, Difficulty Level - M

17.9 Typical victims of chronic bronchitis are invariably:

(A) male
(B) over 40
(C) heavy cigarette smokers
(D) nutritionally deficient

*Answer: C, Page: 292, Difficulty Level - M

17.10 The term "blue bloaters" refers to victims of:

(A) dyspnea
(B) emphysema
(C) chronic bronchitis
(D) asthma

*Answer: C, Page: 293, Difficulty Level - M

17.11 Which of the following is <u>not</u> a sign or symptom of chronic bronchitis?

(A) cyanosis
(B) distended neck veins
(C) high-pitched wheezing
(D) pinkish coloring

*Answer: D, Page: 293, Difficulty Level - M

17.12 Coughing that produces thick mucus; swelling of the hands, feet and ankles; and low-pitched snoring sounds during inhalation and exhalation, are all signs and symptoms of:

(A) emphysema
(B) chronic bronchitis
(C) asthma
(D) pneumonia

*Answer: B, Page: 293, Difficulty Level - M

17.13 The number one goal of emergency care for COPD is to:

(A) enhance oxygenation
(B) loosen restrictive clothing
(C) increase circulation
(D) none of the above

*Answer: A, Page: 293, Difficulty Level - E

17.14 A reaction to dust or pollen, often seasonal and occurs most often in children, describes which of the following types of asthma?

(A) intrinsic
(B) acute
(C) extrinsic
(D) status asthmaticus

*Answer: C, Page: 293, Difficulty Level - M

17.15 Which of the following is <u>not</u> indicative of asthma?

(A) a mucus producing cough
(B) rapid, shallow respirations
(C) whistling, high-pitched wheezing during exhalation
(D) rapid pulse

*Answer: A, Page: 294, Difficulty Level - M

17.16 Which of the following is <u>not</u> a reliable sign of status asthmaticus?

(A) dehydration
(B) bluish discoloration of the skin
(C) exhaustion
(D) wheezing

*Answer: D, Page: 294, Difficulty Level - C

17.17 A sever, prolonged asthma attack that does not respond to aggressive treatment is:

(A) acute asthma
(B) intrinsic asthma
(C) extrinsic asthma
(D) status asthmaticus

*Answer: D, Page: 294, Difficulty Level - M

17.18 Which of the following is <u>not</u> part of the emergency care of an asthma victim?

(A) keep the victim in a position of comfort
(B) refrain from giving the victim anything by mouth
(C) keep the victim as calm as possible
(D) activate the EMS system

*Answer: B, Page: 294, Difficulty Level - C

17.19 The signs and symptoms of pneumonia depend on:

(A) the age of the victim
(B) the medical history of the victim
(C) what caused the pneumonia
(D) the lobe of the lung that is affected

*Answer: D, Page: 296, Difficulty Level - M

17.20 Which of the following is a sign or symptom of pneumonia?

(A) a dry, unproductive cough
(B) cold, moist skin
(C) chest pain
(D) all of the above

*Answer: C, Page: 296, Difficulty Level - M

17.21 A fever usually exceeding 101 degrees F. and chills that "shake the bed" are symptoms of:

(A) pneumonia
(B) status asthmaticus
(C) chronic bronchitis
(D) none of the above

*Answer: A, Page: 296, Difficulty Level - M

17.22 The causes of hyperventilation syndrome usually involve:

(A) fatigue
(B) anxiety and stress
(C) over-exertion
(D) none of the above

*Answer: B, Page: 296, Difficulty Level - M

17.23 "Over breathing" is associated with which one of the following conditions?

(A) pneumonia
(B) asthma
(C) hyperventilation
(D) emphysema

*Answer: C, Page: 296, Difficulty Level - M

17.24 Which of the following is a sign or symptom of hyperventilation syndrome?

(A) blurring of vision
(B) abdominal discomfort or bloating
(C) tightness or a "lump" in the throat
(D) all of the above

*Answer: D, Page: 296, Difficulty Level - M

17.25 Which of the following is not proper emergency care for a victim with hyperventilation?

(A) remain calm and assuring
(B) have the victim breathe into a paper bag
(C) transport the victim to an emergency room
(D) talk the victim into slowing the breathing rate

*Answer: B, Page: 297, Difficulty Level - M

17.26 Hyperventilation involves breathing at a rate faster than:

(A) 25
(B) 30
(C) 40
(D) none on the above

*Answer: C, Page: 296, Difficulty Level – M

TRUE / FALSE

17.27 Without enough oxygen, certain cells in the body can die within minutes.

*Answer: True, Page: 290, Difficulty Level - E

17.28 More than 90 percent of those with chronic obstructive pulmonary disease have emphysema, chronic bronchitis or both.

*Answer: True, Page: 291, Difficulty Level - M

17.29 Because victims of emphysema are usually cyanotic, they are referred to as "blue bloaters".

*Answer: False, Page: 291, Difficulty Level - M

17.30 The most important known factor in COPD is cigarette smoking.

*Answer: True, Page: 292, Difficulty Level - E

17.31 The victim of emphysema usually has a tendency toward associated heart disease and right-heart failure.

*Answer: False, Page: 292, Difficulty Level - C

17.32 When caring for a victim with asthma, give the victim as much fluid by mouth as possible unless you anticipate vomiting.

*Answer: True, Page: 294, Difficulty Level – M

17.33 It is important to stay calm when caring for a victim with asthma, because stress and emotional intensity can actually worsen the asthma.

*Answer: True, Page: 294, Difficulty Level - M

17.34 You can safely assume that a wheezing victim has asthma.

*Answer: False, Page: 294, Difficulty Level - M

17.35 Overbreathing increases the carbon dioxide in the blood to an abnormal level, causing hyperventilation.

*Answer: False, Page: 296, Difficulty Level - C

17.36 The three goals of emergency care for asthma are to improve oxygenation, relieve bronchospasm and improve the victim's ventilation.

*Answer: True, Page: 297, Difficulty Level - C

CHAPTER EIGHTEEN
DIABETIC EMERGENCIES

MULTIPLE CHOICE

18.1 Conservatively estimated, there are more than __________ diabetics in the United States.

(A) 5 million
(B) 10 million
(C) 14 million
(D) 18 million

*Answer: C, Page: 302, Difficulty Level - C

18.2 Approximately, how many of all diabetics go undiagnosed or recognized?

(A) one-fourth
(B) half
(C) three-fourths
(D) none of the above

*Answer: B, Page: 302, Difficulty Level - M

18.3 Insulin is a hormone needed to facilitate the movement of __________ out of the bloodstream and into the cell.

(A) iron
(B) carbon dioxide
(C) sugar
(D) oxygen

*Answer: C, Page: 303, Difficulty Level - M

18.4 In diabetes, __________ accumulates in the bloodstream.

(A) sugar
(B) bacteria
(C) abnormal cells
(D) insulin

*Answer: A, Page: 303, Difficulty Level - M

18.5 During normal digestion, insulin is released by the:

(A) liver
(B) spleen
(C) small intestines
(D) pancreas

*Answer: D, Page: 303, Difficulty Level - M

18.6 When the cells of the body don't get the glucose they need, _______ are used as fuel instead.

(A) proteins
(B) acids
(C) fats
(D) all of the above

*Answer: A, Page: 303, Difficulty Level - M

18.7 Which of the following is a common complication from diabetes?

(A) blindness
(B) circulatory problems
(C) sexual dysfunction
(D) all of the above

*Answer: D, Page: 303, Difficulty Level - M

18.8 Which of the following is not characteristic of type I diabetes?

(A) the victim has little or no ability to produce insulin
(B) it is generally controlled by diet and/or oral medication
(C) it usually begins in childhood
(D) victims require daily insulin injections

*Answer: B, Page: 304, Difficulty Level - M

18.9 Diabetics face a grave physical situation when their blood glucose level is:

(A) too high
(B) too low
(C) too high or two low

*Answer: C, Page: 304, Difficulty Level - M

18.10 All of the following are signs and symptoms of hypoglycemia except:

(A) headache
(B) intense thirst
(C) pale, moist skin
(D) dizziness, faintness

*Answer: B, Page: 305, Difficulty Level - C

18.11 Hypoglycemia is also known as:

(A) diabetic coma
(B) type I diabetics
(C) diabetic ketoacidosis
(D) insulin shock

*Answer: D, Page: 307, Difficulty Level - M

18.12 Which of the following would most likely be a cause of hyperglycemia?

(A) excessive exercise
(B) too much insulin taken
(C) eating too much food containing sugar
(D) not eating enough or at all

*Answer: C, Page: 306, Difficulty Level - M

18.13 All of the following are signs and symptoms of hyperglycemia except:

(A) fever
(B) frequent urination
(C) breath that smells sweet or fruity
(D) absence of thirst

*Answer: D, Page: 306, Difficulty Level - C

18.14 A general rule about emergency care for diabetics is; when in doubt:

(A) give insulin
(B) give sugar
(C) do not give sugar
(D) do not give insulin

*Answer: B, Page: 305, Difficulty Level - E

18.15 A condition that results from too little insulin and too much sugar is:

(A) diabetic coma
(B) type II diabetes
(C) hypoglycemia
(D) insulin shock

*Answer: A, Page: 306, Difficulty Level - M

18.16 Which of the following might be a sign that an unconscious victim is diabetic?

(A) poor circulation or amputation of the toes
(B) injection needles
(C) a medical alert tag
(D) all of the above

*Answer: D, Page: 304, Difficulty Level - M

18.17 The onset of hypoglycemia is:

(A) gradual, over the period of days
(B) with in twelve to twenty-four hours
(C) sudden, within minutes
(D) nonc of the above

*Answer: C, Page: 306, Difficulty Level - M

18.18 Which of the following is a sign or symptom of hyperglycemia:

(A) flushed, dry, warm skin
(B) paralysis on one side of the body
(C) speech difficulties
(D) pale, moist skin

*Answer: A, Page: 306, Difficulty Level - C

18.19 When caring for a conscious victim of insulin shock, after activating the EMS system you should:

(A) give the victim insulin
(B) give the victim sugar
(C) administer artificial ventilation
(D) treat for shock

*Answer: B, Page: 307, Difficulty Level - M

18.20 Which If the following should you avoid when caring for a victim of insulin shock?

(A) giving liquids to an unconscious victim
(B) giving sugar to a conscious victim
(C) spreading the contagious disease
(D) all of the above

*Answer: A, Page: 307, Difficulty Level - M

18.21 What is the best position for a victim of insulin shock?

(A) prone
(B) supine
(C) anatomical
(D) lateral recumbent

*Answer: D, Page: 307, Difficulty Level - C

18.22 A victim of diabetic coma may appear:

(A) intoxicated
(B) symptomless
(C) unconscious
(D) none of the above

*Answer: A, Page: 307, Difficulty Level - M

18.23 The breath of a victim on insulin shock will have:

(A) a fruity odor
(B) no unusual odor
(C) an odor of acetone
(D) an odor of alcohol

*Answer: B, Page: 308, Difficulty Level - M

18.24 Which of the following is a life-threatening emergency?

(A) diabetic coma
(B) insulin shock
(C) A & B
(D) none of the above

*Answer: C, Page: 308, Difficulty Level - M

18.25 All of the following are true about gestational diabetes <u>except</u>:

(A) it can almost always be treated with diet
(B) it ends when the baby is born
(C) women with gestational diabetes tend to deliver smaller than normal babies
(D) all of the above are true

*Answer: C, Page:304, Difficulty Level – E

TRUE / FALSE

18.26 The first indication of diabetes may be a life-threatening emergency.

*Answer: True, Page: 302, Difficulty Level - M

18.27 Type I diabetes is often called "adult-onset" diabetes.

*Answer: False, Page: 304, Difficulty Level - M

18.28 You should always make certain to distinguish between insulin shock a diabetic coma before administering sugar.

*Answer: False, Page: 305, Difficulty Level - M

18.29 Insulin shock is a grave medical emergency that can cause death in minutes.

*Answer: True, Page: 308, Difficulty Level - M

18.30 A symptom of diabetic coma is pale, moist skin.

*Answer: False, Page: 307, Difficulty Level - C

18.31 The victim of a diabetic coma will usually complain of dry mouth and intense thirst.

*Answer: True, Page: 307, Difficulty Level - C

18.32 Honey, jelly, lifesavers and orange juice can all be given to a victim of insulin shock to help increase the blood sugar level.

*Answer: True, Page; 308, Difficulty Level - E

18.33 Type II diabetes requires the victim to have an insulin injection daily.

*Answer: False, Page: 308, Difficulty Level - M

18.34 Gestational diabetes increases a woman's risk of developing type II diabetes later in life.

*Answer:True, Page:304, Difficulty Level - M

CHAPTER NINETEEN
ACUTE ABDOMINAL DISTRESS AND RELATED EMERGENCIES

MULTIPLE CHOICE

19.1 Abdominal pain should be considered especially serious if the pain is associated with:

(A) lowered blood pressure
(B) fainting
(C) a toxic appearance
(D) all of the above

*Answer: C, Page: 312, Difficulty Level - M

19.2 In assessing a victim with acute abdominal distress, the number one priority should be to look for signs of:

(A) shock
(B) bleeding
(C) respiratory distress
(D) none of the above

*Answer: A, Page: 313, Difficulty Level - M

19.3 It is typical for a victim with acute abdominal distress to:

(A) be violent
(B) guard
(C) bleed profusely
(D) all of the above

*Answer: B, Page: 313, Difficulty Level - M

19.4 If you know that a specific quadrant is causing the pain or the majority of the pain, examine the quadrant:

(A) first
(B) last
(C) either first or last, it doesn't make a difference

*Answer: B, Page: 314, Difficulty Level - M

19.5 Which of the following is not one of the signs and symptoms of acute abdominal distress?

(A) nausea and /or vomiting
(B) rapid shallow breathing
(C) high blood pressure
(D) colicky pain

*Answer: C, Page: 314, Difficulty Level - M

19.6 How many causes of abdominal pain are there according to medical reference guides?

(A) twenty-five
(B) fifty
(C) one hundred
(D) two hundred

*Answer: C, Page: 312, Difficulty Level - C

19.7 All of the following are priorities when caring for victims of acute abdominal distress in the field except:

(A) assessing injuries
(B) rendering appropriate emergency care
(C) transport
(D) trying to isolate the cause of the abdominal distress

*Answer: D, Page: 312, Difficulty Level - M

19.8 The stomach, spleen, liver and pancreas would all be found in which of the four abdominal quadrants?

(A) left upper
(B) left lower
(C) right upper
(D) right lower

*Answer: A, Page: 313, Difficulty Level - M

19.9 Which of the following organs would be in the abdominal right, lower quadrant?

(A) liver, spleen, pancreas
(B) colon, appendix, small intestines
(C) gallbladder, pancreas, liver
(D) none of the above

*Answer: B, Page: 313, Difficulty Level - M

19.10 If the victim of acute abdominal distress is a child and there is tenderness or guarding on palpation.

(A) suspect the need for surgery
(B) it could be only growing pains
(C) suspect internal bleeding
(D) none of the above

*Answer: A, Page: 314, Difficulty Level - M

19.11 Which of the following is one of the general guidelines for assessment of abdominal injury?

(A) confirm abnormal contour with the victim
(B) determine the quadrant of the pain
(C) look to see whether the abdomen is distended
(D) all of the above

*Answer: D, Page: 314, Difficulty Level - C

19.12 A victim of acute abdominal distress should determine the most comfortable position for himself unless:

(A) there is internal bleeding
(B) the pain is coming from the upper right quadrant
(C) there are signs of shock
(D) all of the above

*Answer: C, Page: 315, Difficulty Level - M

19.13 If the victim of acute abdominal distress is nauseated you should position him or her:

(A) in an upright position
(B) on the left side
(C) on the right side
(D) on his or her back with head slightly elevated

*Answer: B, Page: 315, Difficulty Level - C

19.14 Which of the following should you never do when caring for victims of acute abdominal distress?

(A) give them food
(B) give them water
(C) give them medication
(D) all of the above

*Answer: D, Page: 315, Difficulty Level - M

19.15 Colicky pain is described as a cramp like pain that occurs:

(A) without warning
(B) starting at the head and moving
(C) in waves
(D) in adolescents

*Answer: C, Page: 314, Difficulty Level - C

19.16 A victim of acute abdominal distress will have pain that:

(A) is localized
(B) is diffuse
(C) can be relieved with medication
(D) can be local or diffuse

*Answer: D, Page: 314, Difficulty Level - C

19.17 The best position for a victim of shock is:

(A) on his or her back with legs slightly elevated
(B) on his or her back with head slightly elevated
(C) on either side
(D) none of the above

*Answer: A, Page: 315, Difficulty Level - C

19.18 Esophageal varices are common among:

(A) heavy alcohol drinkers
(B) victims of jaundice
(C) victims of liver disease
(D) all of the above

*Answer: D, Page: 317, Difficulty Level - M

19.19 Ruptured esophageal varices are usually characterized by:

(A) painful gastrointestinal bleeding
(B) painless gastrointestinal bleeding
(C) high fever & flushed appearance
(D) a dry, hacking cough

*Answer: B, Page: 317, Difficulty Level - M

19.20 Victims of ruptured esophageal varices usually have __________ pain in the stomach.

(A) no
(B) localized
(C) extreme
(D) cramping

*Answer: A, Page: 317, Difficulty Level - M

19.21 The victim of ruptured esophageal varices needs rapid blood replacement and surgical procedures aimed at:

(A) repairing the esophagus
(B) opening the airway
(C) stopping the bleeding
(D) none of the above

*Answer: C, Page: 317, Difficulty Level - C

19.22 An abdominal aortic aneurysm is most common in those with:

(A) a liver disease
(B) atherosclerosis
(C) arteriosclerosis

*Answer: B, Page: 317, Difficulty Level - M

19.23 It is estimated that ________ percent of all men over the age of fifty have abdominal aortic aneurysms.

(A) 5
(B) 10
(C) 20
(D) 50

*Answer: C, Page: 317, Difficulty Level - C

19.24 The pain from abdominal aortic aneurysm that ruptures is:

(A) severe
(B) sudden
(C) constant
(D) all of the above

*Answer: D, Page: 317, Difficulty Level - M

19.25 All of the following are signs and symptoms of a ruptured abdominal aortic aneurysm except:

(A) pale legs
(B) mottled abdominal skin
(C) pain in the abdomen
(D) increased pulse in the groin and foot

*Answer: D, Page: 317, Difficulty Level - C

19.26 If the aneurysm has burst, you will feel:

(A) a soft abdomen
(B) a hard, rigid abdomen
(C) a pulsating abdominal mass
(D) none of the above

*Answer: B, Page: 318, Difficulty Level - M

TRUE / FALSE

19.27 Abdominal distress of every victim should be considered life-threatening until proven otherwise.

*Answer: True, Page: 312, Difficulty Level - M

19.28 The upper and lower quadrants are differentiated at the navel.

*Answer: True, Page: 313, Difficulty Level - E

19.29 A victim with acute abdominal distress will appear to be fine.

*Answer: False, Page: 314, Difficulty Level - E

19.30 In a victim with abdominal pain, do not waste time with extensive palpation of the abdomen - it can worsen the pain and aggravate the medical condition that causes it.

*Answer: True, Page: 314, Difficulty Level - M

19.31 A victim with acute abdominal distress often adopts a position on his or her side with knees drawn up toward the abdomen.

*Answer: True, Page: 314, Difficulty Level - E

19.32 Only give liquids to a victim of acute abdominal distress to prevent dehydration.

*Answer: False, Page: 315, Difficulty Level - M

19.33 A victim of acute abdominal distress must always be transported, because many need surgery.

*Answer: True, Page: 315, Difficulty Level - M

19.34 When esophageal varices rupture, bleeding can be fatal within minutes.

*Answer: True, Page: 317, Difficulty Level - M

19.35 A victim with ruptured esophageal varices should be positioned on his or her side with the face pointed downward.

*Answer: True, Page: 317, Difficulty Level - M

19.36 When an abdominal aortic aneurysm ruptures, your primary goal is to prevent bleeding.

*Answer: False, Page: 317, Difficulty Level - C

CHAPTER TWENTY
EPILEPSY, DIZZINESS, AND FAINTING

MULTIPLE CHOICE

20.1 A seizure is an involuntary, sudden change in:

(A) sensation
(B) muscle activity
(C) level of consciousness
(D) any of the above

*Answer: D, Page: 323, Difficulty Level - M

20.2 Which of the following causes of seizures is a derangement in the body's chemistry, and accounts for 10 to 15 percent of all seizures?

(A) toxic
(B) metabolic
(C) idiopathic
(D) vascular

*Answer: B, Page: 323, Difficulty Level - M

20.3 A seizure that usually occurs in young children in conjunction with a fever is:

(A) degenerative
(B) febrile
(C) vascular
(D) metabolic

*Answer: B, Page: 323, Difficulty Level - M

20.4 A toxic seizure occurs as a direct consequence of:

(A) an allergic reaction to drugs or withdrawal from addicting substances
(B) a previous injury to the brain
(C) an inflammation of the brain
(D) derangements in the body's chemistry

*Answer: A, Page: 323, Difficulty Level - M

20.5 Most seizures last only as long as:

(A) two minutes
(B) five minutes
(C) ten minutes
(D) twenty minutes

*Answer: B, Page: 325, Difficulty Level - M

20.6 Which of the following is not one of the stages of a grand mal seizure?

(A) the aura
(B) autonomic discharge
(C) the clonic phase
(D) status epilepticus

*Answer: D, Page: 327, Difficulty Level - M

20.7 A seizure that begins with a blank stare, then progresses into chewing and random activity is a:

(A) myoclonic seizure
(B) grand mal seizure
(C) psychomotor seizure
(D) atonic seizure

*Answer: C, Page: 325, Difficulty Level - M

20.8 A seizure in which the legs of a child suddenly and temporarily collapse is a:

(A) psychomotor seizure
(B) Jacksonian seizure
(C) atonic seizure
(D) infantile seizure

*Answer: C, Page: 325, Difficulty Level - M

20.9 The postseizure phase of a grand mal seizure is characterized by:

(A) hyperventilation and rapid heartbeat
(B) the victim lapsing into a coma
(C) extreme muscle rigidity
(D) hallucinations

*Answer: B, Page: 327, Difficulty Level - M

20.10 The phase of a grand mal seizure that lasts fifteen to twenty seconds, where the victim loses consciousness, and stops breathing is called:

(A) the clonic phase
(B) the hypertonic phase
(C) the tonic phase
(D) the post seizure phase

*Answer: C, Page: 325, Difficulty Level - C

20.11 In caring for a victim of a seizure, when should you send for medical help?

(A) if the seizure lasts more than a few minutes
(B) in the victim has more than one seizure
(C) if the victim is a diabetic
(D) all of the above

*Answer: D, Page: 372, Difficulty Level – M

20.12 Which of the following is <u>not</u> appropriate emergency care for a victim of a seizure?

(A) placing padding under the victim's head
(B) removing eye-glasses and loosening tight clothing
(C) turning the victim on his or her left side
(D) putting somcthing between the victim's teeth

*Answer: D, Page: 327, Difficulty Level - M

20.13 When performing a physical assessment on a seizure victim, which of the following should you pay particular attention to?

(A) the level of consciousness
(B) signs of drug or alcohol abuse
(C) fever
(D) all of the above

*Answer: D, Page: 327, Difficulty Level - M

20.14 The number-one goal in caring for a victim who experiences status epilepticus is:

(A) oxygenation
(B) preventing injury
(C) immobilization
(D) none of the above

*Answer: A, Page: 328, Difficulty Level - M

20.15 Which one of the following presents a dire medical emergency?

(A) a grand mal seizure
(B) status epilepticus
(C) a petit mal seizure
(D) all of the above

*Answer: B, Page: 328, Difficulty Level - M

20.16 Which one of the following is the best position for a victim of a seizure?

(A) lying flat on his or her back
(B) on his or her back with head slightly elevated
(C) on his or her left side with face pointed downward
(D) on his or her right side with the face pointed downward

*Answer: C, Page: 328, Difficulty Level - M

20.17 Which one of the following is <u>not</u> proper procedure when caring for a victim of a seizure?

(A) restrain the victim to prevent injury
(B) cover the victim with a blanket to preserve warmth
(C) speak slowly and calmly in a normal tone of voice
(D) ask bystanders to leave to keep the victim from becoming a spectacle

*Answer: A, Page: 328, Difficulty Level - M

20.18 True vertigo involves:

(A) light-headedness
(B) the feeling of being in a dream
(C) a hallucination of motion
(D) wooziness

*Answer: C, Page: 329, Difficulty Level - M

20.19 Which one of the following is a sign or symptom of central vertigo?

(A) nausea
(B) facial droop
(C) vomiting
(D) pale, moist skin

*Answer: B, Page: 329, Difficulty Level - M

20.20 Which one of the following is <u>not</u> true about labyrinthine vertigo?

(A) it occurs as a disturbance in the inner ear
(B) it is the most common type of vertigo
(C) it is characterized by nausea and a whirling sensation
(D) it is the most serious type of vertigo

*Answer: D, Page: 329, Difficulty Level - M

20.21 All of the following are part of proper emergency care for victims of dizziness, except:

(A) reassure the victim
(B) conduct a thorough assessment to rule out any immediate life-threatening conditions
(C) activate the EMS system
(D) encourage the victim to see a physician

*Answer: C, Page: 330, Difficulty Level - E

20.22 A loss of consciousness that results when the brain is temporarily deprived of adequate oxygen is:

(A) central vertigo
(B) syncope
(C) labyrinthine vertigo
(D) none of the above

*Answer: B, Page: 329, Difficulty Level - M

20.23 Fainting is a symptom of which of the following conditions and diseases?

(A) severe emotion
(B) low blood sugar
(C) irregular heart rhythm
(D) all of the above

*Answer: D, Page: 329, Difficulty Level - M

20.24 You can help prevent syncope by:

(A) seating the victim and having the victim lower the head to knee level
(B) splashing cool water in the victim's face
(C) having the victim move around to increase circulation
(D) all of the above

*Answer: A, Page: 329, Difficulty Level - M

20.25 Do not allow a person who has fainted to:

(A) eat or drink for one hour
(B) sit-up immediately
(C) sleep for a while after
(D) take any medication

*Answer: B, Page: 330, Difficulty Level - M

TRUE / FALSE

20.26 Neurological emergencies involving a disturbance in the chemical or electrical activity of the brain are generally more frightening than they are life-threatening.

*Answer: True, Page: 322, Difficulty Level - M

20.27 A victim who passes from one seizure to another without first regaining consciousness presents a life-threatening medical emergency.

*Answer: True, Page: 322, Difficulty Level - M

20.28 It is the high degree of fever rather than how fast the temperature rises that causes a febrile seizure.

*Answer: False, Page: 323, Difficulty Level - C

20.29 An idiopathic seizure arises from a tumor on the brain.

*Answer: False, Page: 323, Difficulty Level - M

20.30 A myoclonic seizure is characterized by sudden, brief, massive muscle jerks that involve all or part of the body.

*Answer: True, Page: 324, Difficulty Level - C

20.31 A psychomotor seizure is also called a "drop attack".

*Answer: False, Page: 325, Difficulty Level - M

20.32 Anyone who experiences a first-time seizure should be evaluated by a physician.

*Answer: True, Page: 327, Difficulty Level - E

20.33 Dizziness and fainting are not medical conditions, but symptoms of various diseases and injuries.

*Answer: True, Page: 329, Difficulty Level - M

20.34 By knowing how to handle a seizure properly, you can lessen its duration.

*Answer: False, Page: 330, Difficulty Level - M

20.35 The number-one goal in treating status epilepticus is oxygenation.

*Answer: True, Page: 331, Difficulty Level - M

CHAPTER TWENTY-ONE
CHILDBIRTH AND RELATED EMERGENCIES

MULTIPLE CHOICE

21. 1 Which of the following is a function of the placenta?

(A) to provide the fetus with nourishment
(B) absorb fetal waste products
(C) to provide oxygen from the mother's blood
(D) all of the above

*Answer: D Page: 337, Difficulty Level - M

21. 2 Which of the following stages of labor lasts the longest?

(A) dilation
(B) crowning
(C) delivery
(D) delivery of the placenta

*Answer: A, Page: 338, Difficulty Level - M

21. 3 During which stage of labor does the mother experience an uncontrollable urge to push?

(A) dilation
(B) crowning
(C) delivery
(D) delivery of the placenta

*Answer: C, Page: 338, Difficulty Level - M

21. 4 The area of skin between the vagina and the anus is the:

(A) cervix
(B) perineum
(C) bloody show
(D) none of the above

*Answer: B, Page: 338, Difficulty Level - E

21. 5 Which of the following signals the first stage of labor?

(A) the presenting part
(B) the bloody show
(C) crowning
(D) all of the above

*Answer: B, Page: 338, Difficulty Level - M

21. 6 During which stage of labor does the cervix stretch and thin?

(A) dilation
(B) crowning
(C) delivery
(D) none of the above

*Answer: A, Page: 338, Difficulty Level - E

21. 7 Which of the following might indicate an attempted nonmedical abortion rather than a spontaneous one?

(A) cramplike abdominal pain
(B) moderate to severe bleeding
(C) a high fever
(D) passage of tissue

*Answer: C, Page: 340, Difficulty Level - M

21. 8 A seizure during pregnancy often signals:

(A) toxemia
(B) an ectopic-pregnancy
(C) a ruptured uterus
(D) miscarriage

*Answer: A, Page: 340, Difficulty Level - M

21. 9 A condition in which a normally positioned placenta separates from the uterine wall during the last three months of pregnancy is:

(A) placenta previa
(B) ectopic pregnancy
(C) toxemia
(D) abruptio placenta

*Answer: D, Page: 341, Difficulty Level - M

21.10 The leading cause of first trimester maternal deaths is:

(A) toxemia
(B) ectopic pregnancy
(C) spontaneous abortion
(D) abruptio placenta

*Answer: B, Page: 341, Difficulty Level - M

21.11 Which of the following statements about toxemia is not true?

(A) Toxemia is a common condition affecting about one in twenty pregnant women.
(B) Toxemia occurs most frequently in the first three months of pregnancy.
(C) Toxemia is characterized by high blood pressure and swelling in the extremities.
(D) Toxemia is most likely to affect women in their twenties who are pregnant for the first time.

*Answer: B, Page: 342, Difficulty Level - M

21.12 Which one of the following is a sign of eclampsia, the second state of toxemia?

(A) high blood pressure
(B) swelling
(C) convulsions
(D) visual disturbances

*Answer: C, Page: 342, Difficulty Level C

21.13 Which one of the following is not a sign or symptom of a ruptured uterus in most cases?

(A) nausea
(B) constant and severe pain
(C) a tearing sensation in the abdomen
(D) excessive vaginal bleeding

*Answer: D, Page: 342, Difficulty Level - C

21.14 Which of the following might cause the uterus to rupture?

(A) extended or forceful labor
(B) many previous pregnancies
(C) a weak uterine scar
(D) all of the above

*Answer: D, Page: 342, Difficulty Level - M

21.15 When transporting a woman in labor, which of the following should you not do?

(A) keep her lying down
(B) try to delay the delivery until you arrive at a hospital
(C) have the victim bend her knees and spread her thighs to watch for crowning
(D) place a folded blanket under the buttocks and lower back

*Answer: B, Page: 343, Difficulty Level - M

21.16 Delivery of the placenta usually occurs within ________ of the birth.

(A) ten minutes
(B) seconds
(C) thirty minutes
(D) one hour

*Answer: A, Page: 347, Difficulty Level - M

21.17 It is normal for a woman to lose as much as ____________ of blood after giving birth.

(A) one cup
(B) two cups
(C) four cups
(D) one pint

*Answer: B, Page: 347, Difficulty Level - M

21.18 If there is excessive vaginal bleeding following delivery, you should:

(A) pack the vagina
(B) place a napkin over the opening
(C) massage the uterus
(D) none of the above

*Answer: C, Page: 347, Difficulty Level - M

21.19 The first thing you should do to care for the newborn is to:

(A) score the infant using the Apgar System
(B) repeat suctioning
(C) dry and warm the infant
(D) flick the soles of the infant's feet

*Answer: C, Page: 348, Difficulty Level - M

21.20 If the infant's heart rate is less than one hundred beats per minute, provide artificial ventilation at the rate of one breath every:

(A) 3 seconds
(B) second
(C) 5 seconds
(D) none of the above

*Answer: A, Page: 348, Difficulty Level - M

21.21 Which of the following is common in breech births?

(A) meconium passage
(B) prolapsed cord
(C) limb presentation
(D) all of the above

*Answer: D, Page: 349-351, Difficulty Level - M

21.22 Amniotic fluid that is greenish or brownish-yellow is a sign of:

(A) prolapsed cord
(B) meconium passage
(C) a premature birth
(D) a breech birth

*Answer: B, Page: 350, Difficulty Level - M

21.23 The most critical aspect of treatment for meconium passage is to:

(A) suction the baby's nose and mouth
(B) alleviate pressure on the cord
(C) stimulate the infant to breathe
(D) none of the above

*Answer: A, Page: 351, Difficulty Level - M

21.24 Which of the following is true about premature babies?

(A) a premature infant cannot tolerate losing even minute amounts of blood
(B) premature babies are more susceptible to infection
(C) a premature baby will generally be thinner, smaller and redder than a full-term baby
(D) all of the above

*Answer: D, Page: 351, Difficulty Level - M

21.25 Premature babies generally require:

(A) resuscitation
(B) a blood transfusion
(C) chest compressions
(D) all of the above

*Answer: A, Page: 351, Difficulty Level - M

21.26 In prolapsed cord, the best position for the mother is:

(A) head down or buttocks raised
(B) on her left side
(C) lying flat on her back
(D) none of the above

*Answer: A, Page: 349, Difficulty Level - M

TRUE/FALSE

21.27 Childbirth is a normal, natural process - in only a few situations do victims need to be transported rapidly.

*Answer: True, Page: 336, Difficulty Level - M

21.28 The vagina is the organ in which the fetus grows and is responsible for labor and expulsion of the infant.

*Answer: False, Page: 337, Difficulty Level - E

21.29 The expulsion of the mucous plug from the cervix is known as the bloody show.

*Answer: True, Page: 338, Difficulty Level - M

21.30 The first stage of labor may last as long as eighteen hours or more for a woman having her first baby.

*Answer: True, Page: 338, Difficulty Level - M

21.31 Bright lights and loud noises can trigger seizures in a toxemia victim.

*Answer: True, Page: 341, Difficulty Level - M

21.32 Toxemia affects approximately one in ten pregnant women.

*Answer: False, Page: 341, Difficulty Level - C

21.33 As a general guideline, you should not try to transport a mother for delivery if delivery is expected within five minutes.

*Answer: True, Page: 343, Difficulty Level - M

21.34 When transporting a woman in labor have the woman cross her legs to prevent the baby from being born before reaching the hospital.

*Answer: False, Page: 343, Difficulty Level - M

21.35 To prevent explosive delivery, place your fingers on the bony part of the infant's skull and exert very gentle pressure.

*Answer: True, Page: 344, Difficulty Level - M

21.36 Vernix Caseosa is the plasticlike sac of fluid in which the baby floats.

*Answer: False, Page: 346, Difficulty Level - E

21.37 When assisting with a delivery, have the woman take long, deep breaths during Contractions and short, quick breaths between contractions.

*Answer: False, Page: 344, Difficulty Level - M

CHAPTER TWENTY-TWO
PEDIATRIC AND GERIATRIC EMERGENCIES

MULTIPLE CHOICE

22.1 All of the following are true about children in comparison to adults except:

(A) children have smaller airways
(B) a child's head is larger in proportion to its body
(C) children have slower respiratory rates
(D) children have faster heart rates

*Answer: C, Page: 357, Difficulty Level - M

22.2 Which of the following is not general procedure when assessing a child?

(A) be honest about pain
(B) get the most painful parts of the assessment over with first
(C) get as close to the child's eye level as possible
(D) involve the parents as much as possible

*Answer: B, Page: 358, Difficulty Level - M

22.3 You can tell the most about a child's status by:

(A) taking the child's vital signs
(B) asking the child himself
(C) asking the parents and witnesses
(D) your overall impressions of how the child looks and acts

*Answer: D, Page: 358, Difficultly Level - M

22.4 Which pulse should you check in a child to take a pulse quickly?

(A) the brachial pulse
(B) the radial pulse
(C) the carotid pulse
(D) none of the above

*Answer: B, Page: 358, Difficulty Level - M

22.5 A viral infection that causes swelling beneath the glottis and progressive narrowing of the airway is:

(A) epiglottitis
(B) asthma
(C) croup
(D) bronchiolitis

*Answer: C, Page: 359, Difficulty Level - M

22.6 Which one of the following is caused by a bacterial infection?

(A) epiglottitis
(B) asthma
(C) croup
(D) bronchiolitis

*Answer: A, Page: 359, Difficulty Level - C

22.7 Which one of the following is <u>not</u> characteristic of <u>both</u> asthma and bronchiolitis?

(A) rapid pulse
(B) an overly inflated chest
(C) the victim is almost always over the age of one
(D) wheezing

*Answer: C, Page: 361, Difficulty Level - M

22.8 Which one of the following is characterized by coughing with a harsh "seal bark"?

(A) croup
(B) epiglottitis
(C) asthma
(D) bronchiolitis

*Answer: A, Page: 360, Difficulty Level - M

22.9 Which one of the following positions is best for a victim of epiglottitis?

(A) on his or her left side
(B) lying flat on his or her back
(C) sitting or semisitting
(D) lying flat with feet elevated at least twelve inches

*Answer: C, Page: 360, Difficulty Level - M

22.10 You should give plenty of fluids to victims of __________ to help loosen and thin mucus in the air passages?

(A) croup
(B) asthma
(C) epiglottitis
(D) bronchiolitis

*Answer: B, Page: 360, Difficulty Level - C

22.11 Ninety-five percent of cardiac arrests in children are from:

(A) airway obstruction and respiratory arrest
(B) shock
(C) trauma to the head
(D) none of the above

*Answer: A, Page: 361, Difficulty Level - M

22.12 Unlike children, adults rarely have seizures caused by:

(A) meningitis
(B) head injury
(C) oxygen deficiency
(D) fever

*Answer: D, Page: 361, Difficulty Level - M

22.13 The number-one cause of death among infants between one month and one year is:

(A) child abuse and neglect
(B) choking
(C) crib death
(D) meningitis

*Answer: C, Page: 362, Difficulty Level - M

22.14 All of the following are true about sudden infant death syndrome <u>except:</u>

(A) a red blotchiness of the skin is usually apparent
(B) it usually involves infants between the ages of four weeks and seven months
(C) it almost always occurs while the infant is sleeping
(D) there is usually an indication of a struggle

*Answer: D, Page: 362, Difficulty Level - M

22.15 Extended stays at school, constant fatigue, listlessness and delinquency are all signs of which type of abuse?

(A) physical
(B) sexual
(C) neglect
(D) emotional

*Answer: C, Page: 364, Difficulty Level - M

22.16 A child who seems withdrawn, fantasizes, has poor peer relationships and demonstrates infantile behavior has most likely been abused:

(A) sexually
(B) physically
(C) emotionally
(D) by neglect

*Answer: A, Page: 364, Difficulty Level - M

22.17 Which of the following would you do if you suspect abuse?

(A) confront the parents
(B) ask the child to recreate the situation
(C) ask neighbors or relatives
(D) report your suspicions to proper authorities

*Answer: D, Page: 365, Difficulty Level - E

22.18 While the elderly represent only about ten percent of the population, they account for _____ percent of all fatal injuries.

(A) 10
(B) 25
(C) 35
(D) 50

*Answer: B, Page: 366, Difficulty Level - M

22.19 It is important to take into account which of the following factors when assessing an elderly victim?

(A) the victim may be taking a number of medications
(B) the geriatric victim is likely to suffer more than one disease at a time
(C) the elderly become debilitated much more rapidly
(D) all of the above

*Answer: D, Page: 366-367, Difficulty Level - M

22.20 Most cases of pneumonia in the elderly are due to:

(A) infection
(B) aspiration
(C) malnutrition
(D) none of the above

*Answer: B, Page: 366, Difficulty Level - M

22.21 The most common sign of myocardial infarction in a elderly person is:

(A) severe pain
(B) fever
(C) shortness of breath
(D) dyspnea

*Answer: C, Page: 366, Difficulty Level - C

22.22 As many as one in _____ elderly have psychiatric disorders, which can be the cause of some symptoms.

(A) four
(B) ten
(C) twenty
(D) twenty-five

*Answer: A, Page: 366, Difficulty Level - C

22.23 The elderly are more prone to head injury; signs and symptoms of brain compression develop more:

(A) rapidly
(B) slowly
(C) severely
(D) aggressively

*Answer: B, Page: 368, Difficulty Level - M

22.24 Which of the following is a child more susceptible to than an adult?

(A) hypothermia
(B) dehydration
(C) head injury
(D) all of the above

*Answer: D, Page: 369, Difficulty Level - M

TRUE/FALSE

22.25 Children have less blood than an adult and are therefore in greater danger of bleeding to death from a relatively minor wound.

*Answer: True, Page: 357, Difficulty Level - M

22.26 It isn't important to check a child's vital signs as often as you would an adult's, because your overall impression of the child's status can tell more than any one vital sign.

*Answer: False, Page: 358, Difficulty Level - M

22.27 An average eight-year-old breathes forty breaths per minute.

*Answer: False, Page: 358, Difficulty Level - C

22.28 A child's temperature is a much more important warning sign than an adult's because it can change so quickly.

*Answer: True, Page: 358, Difficulty Level - M

22.29 Head injury is more likely in an infant because its head is large in proportion to its body.

*Answer: True, Page: 359, Difficulty Level - M

22.30 Croup is a bacterial infection characterized by a high fever, drooling, difficulty speaking and mouth breathing.

*Answer: False, Page: 360, Difficulty Level - C

22.31 Emergency care for a victim of epiglottitis includes examining the child's throat thoroughly.

*Answer: False, Page: 360, Difficulty Level - M

22.32 If you know what to watch for, crib death can be predicted and prevented.

*Answer: False, Page: 362, Difficulty Level - E

CHAPTER TWENTY-THREE
BITES AND STINGS

MULTIPLE CHOICE

23.1 Most poisonous snakes have which one of the following characteristics?

(A) round pupils
(B) large fangs
(C) an oval-shaped head
(D) all of the above

*Answer: B, Page: 375, Difficulty Level - M

23.2 The severity of a snakebite is gauged by:

(A) the size of the snake
(B) how deep the fangs are injected
(C) how rapidly symptoms develop
(D) how recently the victim has eaten

*Answer: C, Page: 376, Difficulty Level - M

23.3 The pain from a pit viper bite feels:

(A) burning
(B) dull
(C) shooting
(D) sharp

*Answer: A, Page: 376, Difficulty Level - M

23.4 As a general rule, you can safely assume that the victim has not been poisoned by a pit viper bite if pain does not develop within:

(A) ten minutes
(B) one hour
(C) six to eight hours
(D) twenty-four hours

*Answer: B, Page: 376, Difficulty Level - C

23.5 Which of the following are factors that can determine the severity of a snakebite?

(A) the location of the bite
(B) the size and weight of the victim
(C) the general health and condition of the victim
(D) all of the above

*Answer: D, Page: 376, Difficulty Level - M

23.6 All of the following are signs and symptoms of a pit viper bite <u>except</u>:

(A) dimmed vision
(B) muscular twitching
(C) a red rash over the entire body
(D) two distinct fang marks

*Answer: C, Page: 376, Difficulty Level - C

23.7 Which one of the following signs and symptoms is characteristic of a coral snake bite?

(A) purplish discoloration around the bite
(B) blurred vision and drooping eyelids
(C) severe pain and swelling around the bitten area
(D) all of the above

*Answer: B, Page: 376, Difficulty Level - C

23.8 The signs and symptoms of a coral snake bite usually occur:

(A) immediately
(B) within twenty minutes after the bite
(C) between one and eight hours after the bite
(D) within twenty four hours

*Answer: C, Page: 376, Difficulty Level - M

23.9 The wound from a poisonous snakebite is usually:

(A) shallow and slanted
(B) deep and slanted
(C) deep and straight
(D) none of the above

*Answer: A, Page: 377, Difficulty Level - M

23.10 Generally, medical help is needed for an insect bite or sting only if:

(A) itching lasts longer than two days
(B) signs of infection develop
(C) signs of an allergic reaction develop
(D) all of the above

*Answer: D, Page: 378, Difficulty Level - M

23.11 The crimson red marking that characterizes a black widow spider is shaped like:

(A) a star
(B) two dots
(C) an hourglass
(D) an x

*Answer: C, Page: 378, Difficulty Level - E

23.12 Which of the following might be a sign or symptom of a black widow spider bite?

(A) fever and chills
(B) small red fang marks
(C) nausea and vomiting
(D) all of the above

*Answer: D, Page: 378, Difficulty Level - M

23.13 The bite of the brown recluse spider:

(A) is a serious medical condition
(B) does not heal
(C) requires surgical repair
(D) all of the above

*Answer: D, Page: 378, Difficulty Level - M

23.14 Within seven to ten days, the bite of a brown recluse spider:

(A) disappears
(B) becomes a large ulcer
(C) starts to itch unbearably
(D) becomes bluish in color

*Answer: B, Page: 378, Difficulty Level - M

23.15 Ninety percent of all scorpion bites occur on the:

(A) hands
(B) feet
(C) head or face
(D) legs

*Answer: A, Page: 379, Difficulty Level - M

23.16 The severity of a scorpion sting depends on:

(A) how deep it is
(B) how soon symptoms appear
(C) the amount of venom injected
(D) the size of the wound

*Answer: C, Page: 379, Difficulty Level - M

23.17 A sign or symptom of a scorpion sting additional to the general signs and symptoms of insect bites and stings is:

(A) a high fever
(B) abdominal cramping
(C) poor coordination
(D) shortness of breath

*Answer: C, Page: 379, Difficulty Level - C

23.18 The only appropriate pre-hospital treatment for a tick bite is:

(A) a cold compress
(B) to give the victim lots of fluids
(C) prompt removal of the tick
(D) to clean and sanitize around the area

*Answer: C, Page: 379, Difficulty Level - M

23.19 A local reaction from an insect sting can successfully be treated with:

(A) an antibiotic
(B) cold compresses
(C) a heating pad
(D) direct pressure

*Answer: B, Page: 380, Difficulty Level - M

23.20 All of the following are signs and symptoms of anaphylactic shock <u>except</u>:

(A) stiffening of the joints
(B) hives
(C) low blood pressure
(D) generalized itching

*Answer: A, Page: 380, Difficulty Level - C

23.21 Which of the following leave the stinger behind and therefore can sting only once?

(A) wasps
(B) hornets
(C) honeybees
(D) all of the above

*Answer: C, Page: 380, Difficulty Level - M

23.22 An important difference between marine animal bites and land animal bites is that:

(A) the venom of marine life may cause more extensive tissue damage
(B) signs and symptoms of marine animal bites progress much more rapidly
(C) marine animal bites produce permanent damage
(D) all of the above

*Answer: A, Page: 382, Difficulty Level - C

23.23 To which one of the following should you apply a cold compress?

(A) an insect sting
(B) a snakebite
(C) a marine animal injury
(D) all of the above

*Answer: A, Page: 384, Difficulty Level - M

23.24 When caring for a bite or sting the injection site should be:

(A) elevated slightly
(B) even with the victim's heart
(C) elevated at least twelve inches
(D) below the level of the victims heart

*Answer: D, Page: 384, Difficulty Level - M

23.25 For poisonous snakebite apply a constricting band __________ the site of the bite if local protocol advises.

(A) below
(B) above
(C) over

*Answer: B, Page: 384, Difficulty Level - E

23.26 Which of the following should be used for removing a tick?

(A) tweezers
(B) a hot match
(C) petroleum jelly
(D) rubbing alcohol

*Answer: A, Page:386, Difficulty Level – E

TRUE/FALSE

23.27 The coral snake is a poisonous snake, but does not have the usual fangs or a pit.

*Answer: True, Page: 375, Difficulty Level - M

23.28 The location of a snakebite influences its severity because fatty tissue absorbs venom more rapidly than muscle tissue.

*Answer: False, Page: 376, Difficulty Level - M

23.29 A minty, metallic or rubbery taste in the mouth is a sign or symptom of a pit viper bite.

*Answer: True, Page: 376, Difficulty Level - M

23.30 Black widow spider bites are the leading cause of death from spider bites in the United States.

*Answer: True, Page: 378, Difficulty Level - M

23.31 Most brown recluse spider bite victims are unaware they have been bitten because the bite is often painless at first.

*Answer: True, Page: 378, Difficulty Level - M

23.32 The bite of the black widow spider is especially serious because the bite does not heal and requires surgical repair.

*Answer: False, Page: 378, Difficulty Level – M

23.33 Tick bites are serious because they carry meningitis.

*Answer: False, Page: 379, Difficulty Level - E

23.34 Anaphylactic shock may cause death within minutes.

*Answer: True, Page: 380, Difficulty Level - M

23.35 You should encourage a victim to move around after a bite or sting to keep the joints from stiffening.

*Answer: False, Page: 384, Difficulty Level - M

23.36 Marine life venom is destroyed by heat rather than cold.

*Answer: True, Page: 386, Difficulty Level - M

CHAPTER TWENTY-FOUR
BURN EMERGENCIES

MULTIPLE CHOICE

24.1 Burns are classified by:

(A) the location of the burn
(B) the degree of damage to the skin and underlying tissue
(C) the percentage of the body burned
(D) the age of the victim

*Answer: B, Page: 391, Difficulty Level - M

24.2 A burn that involves both the epidermal and dermal layer of skin, characterized by blistering, swelling and pain is a:

(A) first-degree burn
(B) second-degree burn
(C) third-degree burn

*Answer: B, Page: 391, Difficulty Level - M

24.3 A method for determining quickly the percentage of the body that has been burned is:

(A) the Rule of Nines
(B) burn classification
(C) the palmer surface method
(D) A & C

*Answer: D, Page: 393, Difficulty Level - M

24.4 Skin that is moist and mottled ranging from white to cherry red with blisters, would be classified as a:

(A) first-degree burn
(B) second-degree burn
(C) third-degree burn

*Answer: B, Page: 393, Difficulty Level - M

24.5 A first-degree burn usually takes ___________ days to heal.

(A) two to five
(B) five to ten
(C) ten to twenty
(D) more than twenty

*Answer: A, Page: 393, Difficulty Level - M

24.6 Which of the following would likely cause a full-thickness burn?

(A) electricity
(B) chemicals
(C) hot grease
(D) all of the above

*Answer: D, Page: 395, Difficulty Level - M

24.7 Burns on the face or neck should be seen by a physician immediately because:

(A) they don't heal well
(B) they are almost always third-degree burns
(C) of possible burns to the eyes
(D) they will need cosmetic surgery

*Answer: C, Page: 395, Difficulty Level - M

24.8 In an elderly patient, a burn covering only ________ percent of the body can often by fatal.

(A) 10
(B) 20
(C) 30
(D) less than 10

*Answer: B, Page: 395, Difficulty Level - M

24.9 Children under five and adults over sixty react more severely to a burn because:

(A) they have extremely thin skin
(B) they have a disproportionate fluid-to-surface-area ratio
(C) their immunity is incomplete or compromised
(D) all of the above

*Answer: D, Page: 395-396, Difficulty Level - M

24.10 The most common type of burn is:

(A) chemical
(B) electrical
(C) thermal or radiant
(D) none of the above

*Answer: C, Page: 397, Difficulty Level - M

24.11 When caring for a burn victim, if the skin is not broken, less than 10 percent of the body surface is burned, and the victim is in a cold environment, you should:

(A) cover the burned area with cool, wet compresses
(B) apply grease or fat to the burn
(C) apply an ice pack to the burned area
(D) leave the burn uncovered to cool in the open air

*Answer: A, Page: 397, Difficulty Level - M

24.12 Swelling of the respiratory tissues following a burn can cause:

(A) the victim to choke
(B) damage to the lungs
(C) the vital signs to change suddenly
(D) the victim to go unconscious

*Answer: C, Page: 397, Difficulty Level - C

24.13 More than half of all fire-related deaths are caused by:

(A) forest fires
(B) third-degree burns
(C) secondary infections from the burn
(D) smoke inhalation

*Answer: D, Page: 399, Difficulty Level - M

24.14 The most common burn-associated inhalation injury is:

(A) heat inhalation
(B) inhalation of carbon monoxide
(C) inhalation of toxic chemicals
(D) inhalation of smoke

*Answer: B, Page: 399, Difficulty Level - M

24.15 You should suspect inhalation injury if the victim has:

(A) a sooty or smoky smell on the breath
(B) singed nasal hairs
(C) burned specks of carbon in the saliva
(D) all of the above

*Answer; D, Page: 399, Difficulty Level - E

24.16 Burns usually do not alter levels of consciousness, so you should assume that any victim who is unconscious is suffering from:

(A) respiratory distress
(B) heart failure
(C) carbon monoxide poisoning
(D) none of the above

*Answer: C, Page: 400, Difficulty Level - M

24.17 Every victim of chemical burns should be:

(A) treated for shock
(B) transported to the hospital
(C) given artificial ventilation
(D) suspected of foul play

*Answer: B, Page: 401, Difficulty Level - M

24.18 Before you begin care of a victim of chemical burns you should always:

(A) activate the EMS system
(B) clear bystanders from the area
(C) make sure it is safe to approach the victim
(D) get the victim's consent

*Answer: C, Page: 401, Difficulty Level - M

24.19 The most important treatment for a chemical burn is to:

(A) apply cool compresses
(B) flush the burned area with water
(C) elevate the burned area above the level of the heart
(D) cleanse the area with alcohol

*Answer: B, Page: 401, Difficulty Level - M

24.20 When approaching a vehicle accident that involves downed power lines you should:

(A) carefully move the downed wires
(B) notify the power company and request an emergency crew
(C) help the victim get out of the vehicle immediately
(D) call to the victim to get out of the vehicle

*Answer: B, Page: 403, Difficulty Level - M

24.21 If you find a victim in a bathtub with an electrical appliance that has energized the water, you should;

(A) immediately remove the appliance
(B) remove the victim from the water
(C) drain the water from the bathtub
(D) unplug the appliance before doing anything

*Answer: D, Page: 403, Difficulty Level - M

24.22 A factor that would determine the severity of electrical shock is:

(A) the amount of moisture on the victim
(B) the amount of time the victim was exposed to the shock
(C) the area of the body through which the current passed
(C) all of the above

*Answer: D, Page: 403, Difficulty Level - M

24.23 Always assume that a victim of lightning strike:

(A) has sustained multiple injuries
(B) is still electrically charged
(C) is in shock
(D) has sustained damage to brain cells

*Answer: A, Page: 404, Difficulty Level - M

TRUE/FALSE

24.24 The number of productive years lost to burns is greater than those lost to cancer, heart disease and strokes.

*Answer: True, Page: 390, Difficulty Level - M

24.25 A second-degree burn involves all layers of the skin as well as fat, muscle and bone.

*Answer: False, Page: 391, Difficulty Level - M

24.26 The palmer surface method is a method of using the palm to estimate the percentage of body surface that has been burned.

*Answer: True, Page: 393, Difficulty Level - M

24.27 Any burn to the lower body is more serious than a burn of similar extent and degree on the upper body.

*Answer: False, Page: 395, Difficulty Level - M

24.28 The final result of inhalation of noxious fumes is reduced oxygen exchange.

*Answer: True, Page: 400, Difficulty Level - M

24.29 The current of a contact electrical burn is most intense at the entrance and exit sites.

*Answer: True, Page: 403, Difficulty Level - M

24.30 Victims of lightning strike have a lesser chance of resuscitation than victims of cardiac or respiratory arrest.

Answer: False, Page: 405, Difficulty Level – M

24.31 In caring for a burn, use a plastic dressing to trap moisture to keep the area from drying out.

*Answer: False, Page: 397, Difficulty Level – M

24.32 A tingling sensation in your legs as you approach a victim might indicate that the ground is electrically energized.

*Answer: True, Page:403, Difficulty Level - E

CHAPTER TWENTY-FIVE
HEAT AND COLD EMERGENCIES

MULTIPLE CHOICE

25.1 The loss of body heat involving the transfer of heat from the surface of one object to the surface of another without physical contact is:

(A) radiation
(B) conduction
(C) convection
(D) evaporation

*Answer: A, Page: 411, Difficulty Level - M

25.2 Which of the following would be especially susceptible to heatstroke?

(A) an obese person
(B) an athlete
(C) a person with heart disease
(D) all of the above

*Answer: D, Page: 413, Difficulty Level - M

25.3 <u>All</u> heatstroke victims have:

(A) low blood sugar
(B) compromised levels of consciousness
(C) an unquenchable thirst
(D) extreme fatigue

*Answer: B, Page: 414, Difficulty Level - M

25.4 The body temperature of a victim of heatstroke needs to be cooled below _____ and stay that low before the danger has passed.

(A) 98.6° F
(B) 99.6° F
(C) 100
(D) 101° F

*Answer: C, Page: 416, Difficulty Level - M

25.5 The most critical problem in heat exhaustion is:

(A) muscle cramps
(B) dehydration
(C) a weak, rapid pulse
(D) a below-normal temperature

*Answer: B, Page: 416, Difficulty Level - M

25.6 For which one of the following heat-related emergencies should you have the victim lie down and raise the feet eight to twelve inches?

(A) heatstroke
(B) sunstroke
(C) heat exhaustion
(D) heat cramps

*Answer: C, Page: 417, Difficulty Level - M

25.7 Heat cramps are muscle spasms that occur when:

(A) the body loses too much salt
(B) calcium levels are too high
(C) too much water is consumed
(D) A or C

*Answer: D, Page: 418, Difficulty Level - M

25.8 Emergency care for heat cramps includes administering sips of ______ at the rate of one-half glassful every fifteen minutes.

(A) sugar water
(B) plain water
(C) salt water
(D) lemon-water

*Answer: C, Page: 418, Difficulty Level - M

25.9 In general, the body's thermal control is lost once the body temperature is lowered to:

(A) 95° F
(B) 90 F
(C) 90° F
(D) 85° F

*Answer: A, Page: 419, Difficulty Level - C

25.10 Which is a factor that might contribute to hypothermia even in the absence of cold environment?

(A) the use of drugs
(B) massive blood loss
(C) extremes of age
(D) all of the above

*Answer: D, Page: 419, Difficulty Level - M

25.11 The American Heart Association guidelines suggest attempting CPR on a hypothermia victim, even in the presence of:

(A) fixed and dilated pupils
(B) a very rigid chest wall
(C) lethal injuries
(D) all of the above

*Answer: A, Page: 421, Difficulty Level - M

25.12 You should keep a hypothermia victim in which of the following positions?

(A) semi-sitting
(B) vertical
(C) horizontal
(D) flat with feet elevated

*Answer: C, Page: 421, Difficulty Level - M

25.13 You should do all of the following to prevent further heat loss in a victim of hypothermia, <u>except:</u>

(A) insulate the head
(B) remove wet clothing
(C) move the victim to a warm, sheltered place
(D) insulate the victim from the ground

*Answer: B, Page: 423, Difficulty Level - M

25.14 Severe hypothermia makes the victims appear:

(A) dead
(B) drowsy
(C) cyanotic
(D) to be perspiring

*Answer: A, Page: 423, Difficulty Level – M

25.15 When providing emergency care for sever hypothermia, you should do all of the following <u>except:</u>

(A) assess vital signs over a two-minute period
(B) use mouth to mouth ventilation
(C) try to rewarm the victim by applying heat
(D) insulate the victim against further heat loss

*Answer: C, Page: 423, Difficulty Level - M

25.16 If a victim of immersion hypothermia cannot be rescued from the water immediately, instruct the victim to do all of the following except:

(A) keep head and face out of the water
(B) cross legs under the water
(C) swim around to increase circulation
(D) exert as little as possible

*Answer: C, Page: 423, Difficulty Level - M

25.17 When associated with minimizing heat loss, the E in HELP stands for:

(A) exert
(B) escape
(C) exercise
(D) extremities

*Answer: B, Page: 424, Difficulty Level - C

25.18 You should never thaw the tissue of a victim of frostbite if there is any chance of:

(A) other injuries
(B) refreezing
(C) delayed transport
(D) all of the above

*Answer: B, Page: 426, Difficulty Level – M

25.19 When thawing frostbitten tissue, you should do so:

(A) slowly
(B) with dry heat
(C) by massaging the skin
(D) rapidly

*Answer: D, Page: 426, Difficulty Level - M

25.20 Discolored skin with deep small blisters filled with dark fluid, would be a sign of which degree of frostbite?

(A) first
(B) second
(C) third
(D) fourth

*Answer: C, Page: 426, Difficulty Level - M

TRUE/FALSE

25.21 The windchill factor is a combination of the effects of the speed of the wind and the temperature of the environment.

*Answer: True, Page: 412, Difficulty Level - M

25.22 Classic heatstroke occurs when victims involved in physical exertion and muscle stress retain the ability to sweat.

*Answer: False, Page: 413, Difficulty Level - C

25.23 Pupils that are initially constricted and later dilate are a sign of hypothermia.

*Answer: False, Page: 414, Difficulty Level - C

25.24 Heat exhaustion is actually a mild form of shock brought on by the pooling of blood in the vessels just below the skin.

*Answer: True, Page: 416, Difficulty Level - M

25.25 The primary signs and symptoms of heat exhaustion mimic those of the flu.

*Answer: True, Page: 416, Difficulty Level – M

25.26 Shivering is a response by the body to generate heat. It cannot occur below a body temperature of 95° F.

*Answer: False, Page: 421, Difficulty Level - C

25.27 Cyanosis, facial bloating and slurred speech are all signs and symptoms of hypothermia.

*Answer: True, Page: 422, Difficulty Level - M

25.28 Race can affect the likelihood of frostbite. Blacks are three times more likely to experience frostbite.

*Answer: True, Page: 424, Difficulty Level - M

CHAPTER TWENTY-SIX
WATER EMERGENCIES

MULTIPLE CHOICE

26.1 Drownings account for one in ________ water-related deaths.

(A) three
(B) five
(C) ten
(D) twenty

*Answer: D, Page: 432, Difficulty Level - M

26.2 Recent studies indicate that one-fourth of all infants who drown do so in:

(A) toilets
(B) swimming pools
(C) five-gallon buckets
(D) bathtubs

*Answer: C, Page: 433, Difficulty Level - M

26.3 Autopsies reveal that only about ________ percent of all drowning victims aspirate a significant amount of water.

(A) 5
(B) 15
(C) 20
(D) 30

*Answer: B, Page: 433, Difficulty - C

26.4 The poorest prognosis for drowning victims is for those submerged in:

(A) cold water
(B) deep water
(C) warm water
(D) shallow water

*Answer: C, Page: 434, Difficulty Level - M

26.5 You should never attempt to reach a drowning victim unless you:

(A) have been trained in water-rescue techniques
(B) are wearing a personal flotation device
(C) are accompanied by other rescuers
(D) all of the above

*Answer: D, Page: 435, Difficulty Level - M

26.6 Fifty percent of <u>all</u> drownings occur in:

(A) lakes, rivers or streams
(B) public swimming pools
(C) private swimming pools
(D) bathtubs

*Answer: B, Page: 435, Difficulty Level - M

26.7 When a person dives into cold water, the mammalian diving reflex can prevent:

(A) head injury
(B) shock
(C) death
(D) hypothermia

*Answer: C, Page: 434, Difficulty Level - M

26.8 A large number of adult drownings involve victims:

(A) who thought they were better swimmers than they really were
(B) with detectable levels of blood alcohol
(C) who were trying to save another drowning victim
(D) who were not wearing life preservers

*Answer: B, Page: 435, Difficulty Level - M

26.9 The best way to rescue a conscious drowning victim who is too far away to reach is to:

(A) swim out to where the victim is
(B) throw the victim a life preserver and encourage him to swim to shore
(C) throw out a floating object tied to a rope and tow the victim to shore
(D) none of the above

*Answer: C, Page: 435, Difficulty Level - M

26.10 You should always suspect spinal injury in any swimmer who is:

(A) under eight years old
(B) unconscious
(C) inexperienced
(D) all of the above

*Answer: B, Page: 436, Difficulty Level - M

26.11 ___________ in the airway can cause resistance to ventilations.

(A) Swelling
(B) Muscle spasms
(C) Water
(D) None of the above

*Answer: C, Page: 437, Difficulty Level - M

26.12 When caring for a near-drowning victim, the first thing you should do is:

(A) activate the EMS system
(B) remove the victim from the water
(C) provide artificial ventilations
(D) place the victim on a backboard

*Answer: A, Page: 436, Difficulty Level - M

26.13 If you do not suspect spinal injury in a drowning or near-drowning victim, after removing the victim from the water, place him:

(A) in a semi-sitting position
(B) out flat on his back
(C) on his left side
(D) on a backboard

*Answer: C, Page: 436, Difficulty Level - M

26.14 A near-drowning victim should always be:

(A) treated for shock
(B) given CPR
(C) watched carefully for at least eight hours
(D) taken to a medical facility

*Answer: D, Page: 437, Difficulty Level - M

26.15 Approximately 15 percent of all drowning deaths are due to:

(A) secondary complications
(B) aspiration of water
(C) improper emergency care
(D) spinal injuries

*Answer: A, Page: 437, Difficulty Level - M

26.16 If a drowning or near-drowning victim is not breathing, begin rescue breathing:

(A) as soon as the victim is out of the water
(B) after placing the victim on a backboard
(C) immediately in the water
(D) as soon as additional help arrives

*Answer: C, Page: 438, Difficulty Level - M

26.17 In a diving emergency, you should always assume that even a diver who is conscious:

(A) has multiple fractures
(B) is in cardiac arrest
(C) has aspirated a great deal of water
(D) has spinal injuries

*Answer: D, Page: 439, Difficulty Level - E

26.18 A diving injury in which gases enter the bloodstream is:

(A) decompression sickness
(B) air embolism
(C) barotrauma
(D) none of the above

*Answer: A, Page: 439, Difficulty Level - M

26.19 Which one of the following deep-water diving emergencies have a gradual onset?

(A) air embolism
(B) decompression sickness
(C) barotrauma
(D) all of the above

*Answer: B, Page: 439, Difficulty Level - M

26.20 An emergency that generally occurs because of breath holding is:

(A) barotrauma
(B) air embolism
(C) decompression sickness
(D) coma

*Answer: B, Page: 439, Difficulty Level - M

26.21 All of the following are signs and symptoms of air embolism <u>except</u>:

(A) frothy blood in the nose and mouth
(B) loss or distortion of memory
(C) swelling and crepitus in the neck
(D) inability to void the bladder

*Answer: D, Page: 439, Difficulty Level - C

26.22 Which one of the following water emergencies can cause permanent blindness or deafness if the victim is not immediately cared for at a medical facility?

(A) barotrauma
(B) air embolism
(C) decompression sickness
(D) hypothermia

*Answer: A, Page: 440, Difficulty Level - M

TRUE / FALSE

26.23 "Wet" drowning occurs when a severe muscle spasm of the larynx cuts off respiration but does not allow aspiration of a significant amount of fluid into the lungs.

*Answer: False, Page: 433, Difficulty Level - M

26.24 Generally, you can resuscitate victims who have been submerged in cold water even after thirty minutes.

*Answer: True, Page: 434, Difficulty Level - M

26.25 Panic often contributes to the death of a person who loses self-control in the water.

*Answer: True, Page: 434, Difficulty Level - M

26.26 A near-drowning victim can develop complications and die as long as three of four days after the accident.

*Answer: True, Page: 437, Difficulty Level - M

26.27 Decompression sickness is sometimes referred to as the "squeeze."

*Answer: False, Page: 439, Difficulty Level - E

26.28 Both air embolism and decompression sickness are emergencies that require recompression.

*Answer: True, Page: 440, Difficulty Level - M

26.29 The mammalian diving reflex enables victims in warm water to survive for longer than those in cold water.

*Answer: False, Page: 440, Difficulty Level - M

26.30 You should always assume that a victim of a diving accident has sustained spinal injury, unless the victim is conscious.

*Answer: False, Page: 440, Difficulty Level - M

CHAPTER TWENTY-SEVEN
WILDERNESS EMERGENCIES

MULTIPLE CHOICE

27.1 Most wilderness environmental emergencies are:

(A) life-threatening
(B) preventable
(C) not serious
(D) due to forest fires

*Answer: B, Page: 445, Difficulty Level - M

27.2 The order of the human body's basic physiologic needs are:

(A) food, water, shelter
(B) shelter, food, water
(C) water, shelter, food
(D) shelter, water, food

*Answer: D, Page: 445, Difficulty Level - M

27.3 Without water, a person will die in:

(A) one day
(B) three days
(C) five days
(D) ten days

*Answer: B, Page: 445, Difficulty Level - M

27.4 A normally healthy individual can survive about _____ without food

(A) one week
(B) three days
(C) three weeks
(D) thirty days

*Answer: C, Page: 445, Difficulty Level - M

27.5 When constructing a shelter in the wilderness, the best place is:

(A) in the bottom of a valley or canyon
(B) downwind of a windbreak
(C) one a mountain ridge
(D) none of the above

*Answer: B, Page: 446, Difficulty Level - M

27.6 The best method for purifying water in the wilderness is:

(A) boiling
(B) filtration
(C) purification tablets
(D) chemical additives

*Answer: A, Page: 446, Difficulty Level - M

27.7 Altitude-related illness can occur at altitudes as low as:

(A) 4,000 feet
(B) 5,000 feet
(C) 8,000 feet
(D) 6,000 feet

*Answer: D, Page: 447, Difficulty Level - M

27.8 When caring for a victim of an altitude - related illness, you should first:

(A) have the victim rest
(B) get the victim to a lower elevation
(C) give the victim something to eat
(D) treat for shock

*Answer: B, Page: 448, Difficulty Level - E

27.9 When assessing a victim in the wilderness, you should spend more time on the __________ than you would normally.

(A) primary survey
(B) initial survey
(C) secondary survey
(D) follow-up evaluation

*Answer: C, Page: 448, Difficulty Level - M

27.10 In high altitude pulmonary edema, the body's ability to __________ is diminished.

(A) replace fluids
(B) take in oxygen
(C) pump blood
(D) regulate temperature

*Answer: B, Page: 447, Difficulty Level – M

27.11 All of the following are true about high altitude pulmonary edema <u>except</u>:

(A) it generally starts at 10,000 feet
(B) signs and symptoms develop within a few hours
(C) a victim of HAPE needs immediate medical treatment in a compression chamber
(D) it is caused by reaching a new altitude too quickly

*Answer: B, Page:447, Difficulty Level - M

27.12 When keeping records in the wilderness, the T in the mnemonic C-H-A-R-T means:

(A) treatment
(B) temperature
(C) time
(D) transport

*Answer: D, Page: 449, Difficulty Level - M

27.13 If you have access to the EMS system, you should never try to:

(A) dress wounds yourself
(B) move the victim
(C) replace fluids
(D) perform CPR

*Answer: C, Page: 450, Difficulty Level – C

27.14 Beyond normal treatment of shock, a special consideration for managing shock in a wilderness setting is:

(A) reducing the body's oxygen debt
(B) maintaining the effective circulating volume of blood
(C) maintaining body temperature
(D) controlling bleeding

*Answer: C, Page: 450, Difficulty Level - M

27.15 To prevent infection of a wound in a wilderness setting, irrigate the wound with:

(A) alcohol
(B) povidone iodine
(C) hydrogen peroxide
(D) boiled water

*Answer: D, Page: 450, Difficulty Level - MN

27.16 Which of the following would be a sign or symptom of an infected wound?

(A) redness
(B) hotness
(C) foul order
(D) all of the above

*Answer: D, Page: 450, Difficulty Level - M

27.17 Which one of the following would you do when caring for a fracture in a wilderness setting that you would not normally do in other emergency settings?

(A) splint the fracture
(B) check for signs of impaired circulation
(C) realign an angulated fracture
(D) all of the above

*Answer: C, Page: 451, Difficulty Level – M

27.18 Search and rescue handbooks advise that, depending on the terrain, it requires at least ______ healthy people to carry a body one mile.

(A) four
(B) six
(C) eight
(D) ten

*Answer: C, Page: 452, Difficulty Level - M

27.19 If a victim dies in the wilderness you could do any of the following <u>except:</u>

(A) encase the body in a sleeping bag
(B) wrap the body in a tarp
(C) wrap the body in a tent
(D) wrap the body in a groundcloth

*Answer: A, Page: 452, Difficulty Level - M

27.20 If a victim dies in the wilderness the goal of the first aider is to:

(A) cool the body as rapidly as possible
(B) keep the body warm
(C) bury the body as quickly as possible
(D) notify the next of kin

*Answer: A, Page: 452, Difficulty Level - M

27.21 Which of the following emergency procedures need special consideration in a wilderness setting?

(A) cleaning wounds
(B) reducing fractures
(C) assessment
(D) all of the above

*Answer: D, Page: 452, Difficulty Level – M

TRUE / FALSE

27.22 The higher the altitude, the longer you need to boil the water to destroy all microorganisms effectively.

*Answer: True, Page: 446, Difficulty Level - M

27.23 While eating snow seems a simple way to add water to the body, it carries a high price in terms of heat loss.

*Answer: True, Page: 446, Difficulty Level - M

27.24 The signs and symptoms of acute mountain sickness mimic a severe hangover.

*Answer: True, Page:447, Difficulty Level – M

27.25 Ataxia is a classic sign of high altitude pulmonary edema.

*Answer: False, Page: 448, Difficulty Level - C

27.26 In high altitude cerebral edema, fluid from the body is slowly transferred into the lungs and the body's ability to take on oxygen is diminished.

*Answer: False, Page: 448, Difficulty Level – M

27.27 It is possible for the body to acclimate to higher elevations, but it takes approximately six weeks.

*Answer: True, Page: 447, Difficulty Level - M

27.28 The "Rule of Threes" suggests that you should always go with at least three people into a wilderness setting.

*Answer: False, Page: 445, Difficulty Level - M

27.29 Even though the prognosis for a victim of arrest in the wilderness is grim, you should always begin aggressive CPR as soon as assessment indicates.

*Answer: True, Page: 450, Difficulty Level - M

CHAPTER TWENTY-EIGHT
PSYCHOLOGICAL EMERGENCIES AND DISASTERS

MULTIPLE CHOICE

28.1 Which one of the following is <u>not</u> a basic principle of psychological emergency care?

(A) each person has a right to his or her feelings
(B) every person has limitations
(C) physical trauma is more real than emotional trauma
(D) every person is susceptible to emotional injury

*Answer: C, Page: 458, Difficulty Level - M

28.2 Which one of the following is true concerning psychological emergencies?

(A) hallucinations are usually auditory
(B) the onset of symptoms is sudden
(C) pupils may be dilated
(D) salivation may be excessive

*Answer: A, Page: 459, Difficulty Level - C

28.3 Which of the following is statistically the most at risk for suicide?

(A) a divorced woman over forty
(B) a divorced man over forty
(C) a single woman under forty
(D) a married man under forty

*Answer: B, Page: 462, Difficulty Level - M

28.4 Approximately 80 percent of people who succeed in committing suicide:

(A) had recently lost a loved one
(B) made previous attempts
(C) were overweight
(D) had a recent diagnosis of a serious illness

*Answer: B, Page: 462, Difficulty Level - M

28.5 At highest risk for suicide are victims who have:

(A) a gun
(B) economic trouble
(C) never talked about suicide to anyone
(D) a formulated plan

*Answer: D, Page: 462, Difficulty Level - M

28.6 All of the following are misconceptions about suicide <u>except:</u>

(A) if a person has attempted suicide, he won't do it again
(B) once a persons is suicidal, he's always suicidal
(C) most people who are suicidal can't decide whether to live or die
(D) people who talk about suicide don't commit suicide

*Answer: C, Page: 461, Difficulty Level - M

28.7 When assessing a victim's mental status, ask specific questions that will help you measure:

(A) the victim's level of consciousness
(B) the victim's orientation
(C) the victim's contact with reality
(D) all of the above

*Answer: D, Page: 463, Difficulty Level - C

28.8 When assessing the potential for violence, you should anticipate violence if:

(A) the victim is yelling or cursing
(B) the victim's fists are clenched
(C) the victim is holding anything that could be used as a lethal weapon
(D) any of the above

*Answer: D, Page: 463-464, Difficulty Level - M

28.9 If a victim is obviously dead when you arrive on the scene of a crime, you should:

(A) attempt CPR immediately anyway
(B) gather-up any physical evidence
(C) do nothing and disturb nothing - call the police
(D) attempt to contact family or next of kin

*Answer: C, Page: 465, Difficulty Level - M

28.10 If the victim was strangled and still has the cord or rope around the neck, you should:

(A) untie the knot to remove the rope
(B) leave the rope around the victim's neck
(C) cut the rope to remove the rope
(D) none of the above

*Answer: C, Page: 465, Difficulty Level - M

28.11 One of the best things you can do to protect yourself from legal liability is:

(A) carefully document everything that happens
(B) get a good lawyer
(C) say as little as possible
(D) all of the above

*Answer: A, Page: 465, Difficulty Level - M

28.12 The amount of force considered to be reasonable depends on the victim's:

(A) size
(B) mental state
(C) gender
(D) all of the above

*Answer: D, Page: 465, Difficulty Level - M

28.13 Your first priority in managing a violent victim is to:

(A) confiscate any weapons
(B) put the victim at ease
(C) protect yourself
(D) restrain the victim

*Answer: C, Page: 466, Difficulty Level - M

28.14 When dealing with a disruptive, aggressive victim, you should follow all of the guidelines below except:

(A) identify yourself
(B) speak in short, simple sentences
(C) be overly friendly
(D) adjust your physical distance to a safe range from the victim

*Answer: C, Page: 467, Difficulty Level - M

28.15 If you feel restraining a violent victim is absolutely necessary, approach the victim with at least ______ people.

(A) two
(B) four
(C) six
(D) eight

*Answer: B, Page: 468, Difficulty Level - M

28.16 Which one of the following is not considered a "normal" reaction to a mass casualty or disaster?

(A) extreme anxiety
(B) shakiness
(C) nausea
(D) talking compulsively

*Answer: D, Page: 469, Difficulty Level - C

28.17 A "don't care" attitude would be a sign or symptom of which emotional reaction to a mass casualty:

(A) normal
(B) panic
(C) overactive
(D) underactive

*Answer: D, Page: 469, Difficulty Level - E

28.18 Using the three-level triage method, a victim who is seriously injured and could die without further treatment should be tagged:

(A) delayed
(B) urgent
(C) life-threatened
(D) none of the above

*Answer: B, Page: 471, Difficulty Level - M

28.19 Which of the following would take highest triage priority?

(A) abdominal wounds
(B) burns
(C) major or multiple fractures
(D) obviously mortal wounds

*Answer: A, Page: 471, Difficulty Level - M

28.20 You should not spend more than ______ per victim during actual triage.

(A) 15 to 20 seconds
(B) 30 to 60 seconds
(C) 1 to 2 minutes
(D) 3 to 5 minutes

*Answer: B, Page: 470, Difficulty Level - M

TRUE / FALSE

28.21 A goal of psychological emergency care is to help the injured person begin functioning normally again as soon as possible.

*Answer: True, Page: 457, Difficulty Level - M

28.22 Most persons commit suicide within about 3 months after the beginning of "improvement", when they have the energy to carry out suicidal intentions.

*Answer: True, Page: 461, Difficulty Level - M

28.23 People with terminal illnesses are more likely to commit suicide than those with chronic illnesses.

*Answer: False, Page: 461, Difficulty Level - M

28.24 Sixty to seventy-five percent of all psychological emergency victims will become assaultive or violent.

*Answer: True, Page: 463, Difficulty Level - C

28.25 The basic guideline in using reasonable force is to avoid any act or physical force that may injure the victim during restraint.

*Answer: True, Page: 465, Difficulty Level - M

28.26 When managing a violent victim, negotiate with the victim from a safe distance of at least three feet away.

*Answer: False, Page: 466, Difficulty Level - M

28.27 Three times more women than men attempt suicide, but three times more men are successful.

*Answer: True, Page: 460, Difficulty Level - M

CHAPTER TWENTY-NINE
LIFTING AND MOVING VICTIMS

MULTIPLE CHOICE

29.1 If the scene of an accident is unstable, threatening either your life or the victim's your first priority is:

(A) to quickly perform the ABC's
(B) assessing possible neck or spinal injury
(C) to move the victim
(D) splinting fractures to the neck and back only

*Answer: C, Page: 477, Difficulty Level - M

29.2 If you find a victim in a face-down position, move the victim to an assessment position ________ doing the ABC's.

(A) before
(B) after
(C) while

*Answer: B, Page: 477, Difficulty Level - M

29.3 Under which of the following circumstances should you move a victim?

(A) exposure to hazardous materials
(B) fire
(C) uncontrolled traffic
(D) any of the above

*Answer: D, Page: 477-478, Difficulty Level - E

29.4 If it becomes necessary to move a victim, your speed should depend on:

(A) the reason for the move
(B) the size of the victim
(C) how much the victim is bleeding
(D) how many fractures the victim has sustained

*Answer: A, Page: 477, Difficulty Level - M

29.5 Which one of the following rescue techniques would require two rescuers?

(A) the sheet drag
(B) the extremity lift
(C) the fireman's carry
(D) the walking assist

*Answer: B, Page: 483, Difficulty Level - M

29.6 Unless there is a life-or-death situation, do not attempt a _________ if the victim has suspected spinal injuries or fractures of the extremities.

(A) fireman's carry
(B) shirt drag
(C) blanket drag
(D) sheet drag

*Answer: A, Page: 481, Difficulty Level - M

29.7 To use the sheet drag method, fold the sheet several times lengthwise to form a:

(A) rope
(B) pulley
(C) harness
(D) lasso

*Answer: C, Page: 480, Difficulty Level - E

29.8 Never use which one of the following rescue methods if the victim has back injuries?

(A) the chair litter carry
(B) the extremity lift
(C) seat carries
(D) the blanket drag

*Answer: B, Page: 483, Difficulty Level - C

29.9 The flat lift and carry method of rescue requires _________ rescuer(s).

(A) one
(B) two
(C) three
(D) at least five

*Answer: C, Page: 484, Difficulty Level - M

29.10 A blanket may be used as a stretcher to transport a victim. You should use a blanket that is:

(A) strong
(B) free of holes
(C) large enough to support the victim's entire body
(D) all of the above

*Answer: D, Page: 486, Difficulty Level - M

29.11 When a victim is being carried on a stretcher, he should be transported:

(A) feet-first
(B) head-first
(C) injured-side first
(D) injured-side last

*Answer: A, Page: 489, Difficulty Level - M

29.12 The First Aider at the head of the victim being carried on a stretcher should:

(A) give directions
(B) monitor the victim's condition
(C) carry the majority of the weight
(D) all of the above

*Answer: B, Page: 489, Difficulty Level - M

29.13 If you suspect neck or spinal injuries which of the following methods should you use?

(A) fireman's carry
(B) chair litter carry
(C) extremity lift
(D) none of the above

*Answer: D, Page: 489, Difficulty Level - M

TRUE / FALSE

29.14 Under normal circumstances, a victim should not be moved until a thorough assessment has been made and emergency care has been given.

*Answer: True, Page: 476, Difficulty Level - M

29.15 Under life-threatening conditions, you may have to risk injury to the victim in order to save his or her life.

*Answer: True, Page: 477, Difficulty Level - M

29.16 The shirt drag method works best if the victim is wearing a T-shirt.

*Answer: False, Page: 480, Difficulty Level - E

29.17 The blanket drag method uses a blanket as a harness under the victim's armpits.

*Answer: False, Page: 480, Difficulty Level - M

29.18 You should not use a canvas litter when the victim has to be moved lengthwise.

*Answer: True, Page: 485, Difficulty Level - M

29.19 A good improvised stretcher for an infant or toddler is an infant car seat.

*Answer: True, Page: 486, Difficulty Level - M

CHAPTER THIRTY
VEHICLE STABILIZATION AND VICTIM EXTRICATION

MULTIPLE CHOICE

30.1 When trying to locate all the victim's involved in an accident, you should:

(A) ask coherent passengers how many were in the car
(B) look for tracks
(C) ask witnesses if someone left the site or took victims away
(D) all of the above

*Answer: D, Page: 495, Difficulty Level - M

30.2 If a car is on fire and passengers don't appear to be trapped, you should first:

(A) call for fire-fighting professionals
(B) deal with the fire
(C) move the passengers
(D) warn bystanders to move

*Answer: C, Page: 495, Difficulty Level - M

30.3 If you approach an accident with downed power lines, you should:

(A) rescue the victims from the car
(B) move the downed wires
(C) tell the victims to stay inside the car
(D) call to the victims to leave the car

*Answer: C, Page: 495, Difficulty Level - M

30.4 You should consider any vehicle unstable until:

(A) it is resting on all four wheels
(B) you have made it stable
(C) all victims have been located & extricated
(D) all of the above

*Answer: B, Page: 496, Difficulty Level - M

30.5 Which item would be helpful to have in your first-aid kit to extricate victims in a safe way?

(A) rope
(B) pliers
(C) car jack
(D) all of the above

*Answer: D, Page: 496, Difficulty Level - E

30.6 If you need to gain access to a victim by breaking a window, choose:

(A) the largest one
(B) the one farthest from the victim
(C) the one closest to the victim
(D) one that already is cracked

*Answer: B, Page: 497, Difficulty Level - M

30.7 If the victim does not need to be rescued immediately and a rescue team will be arriving soon, you should:

(A) extricate the victim
(B) control hazards and stabilize the accident scene
(C) give emergency care to stabilize the victim
(D) B & C

*Answer: D, Page: 495, Difficulty Level - M

30.8 If you approach an accident with downed power lines, you should do all of the following <u>except:</u>

(A) park your car a safe distance away
(B) warn bystanders to stay clear
(C) move the wires yourself
(D) call for expert assistance

*Answer: C, Page: 495, Difficulty Level - M

30.9 If the air bag of the car deployed during the accident, expect

(A) neck injuries
(B) harmless cornstarch residue
(C) difficulty in extrication
(D) only minor injuries to the victim

*Answer: D, Page: 496, Difficulty Level - M

30.10 If the vehicle is overturned, place __________ between the roof and the roadway.

(A) a spare tire
(B) timber
(C) cribbing
(D) any of the above

*Answer: D, Page: 496, Difficulty Level - M

30.11 If you have to break a window to gain access to a victim, give a quick, hard thrust in:

(A) the lower corner
(B) center
(C) upper corner
(D) bottom center

*Answer: A, Page: 497, Difficulty Level - M

30.12 Before you crawl through a broken window:

(A) make sure the victim will fit through
(B) drape a tarp or blanket over the edge
(C) pad your knees well
(D) all of the above

*Answer: B, Page: 497, Difficulty Level - M

30.13 If more than one victim is involved:

(A) care for the one closest to you first
(B) care for the youngest first
(C) care for the one who is easiest to extricate first
(D) perform triage

*Answer: D, Page: 497, Difficulty Level - M

30.14 If you have to break a window to gain access to a victim, you should do all of the following <u>except:</u>

(A) put broad strips of tape over the glass before breaking
(B) clear all glass away from the window opening
(C) take time to clean-up the largest pieces of glass to prevent further injury
(D) cover the victim with a blanket as quickly as possible

*Answer: C, Page: 497, Difficulty Level - M

30.15 Once you are inside the car with the victim, you should.

(A) perform the ABC's
(B) complete a rapid primary survey
(C) give psychological support
(D) all of the above

*Answer: D, Page: 497, Difficulty Level - M

30.16 If a victim is found face-down:

(A) turn the victim face-up
(B) do nothing, wait for emergency professionals
(C) give urgent first aid without moving the victim more than necessary
(D) get someone else to help you move the victim

*Answer: C, Page: 498, Difficulty Level - M

TRUE / FALSE

30.17 In most cases, a victim will not have to be moved from a car immediately, you will be able to wait for an emergency team to arrive.

*Answer: True, Page: 495, Difficulty Level - M

30.18 You should assume that all downed power lines are live and call for expert assistance.

*Answer: True, Page: 495, Difficulty Level - M

30.19 You should wait to bandage wounds and splint fractures until after you have moved the victim from a vehicle.

*Answer: False, Page: 497, Difficulty Level

30.20 Extricate means to prioritize the victims for emergency care according to the seriousness of the injuries.

*Answer: False, Page: 495, Difficulty Level - E

30.21 Stabilize a standard transmission vehicle by putting the transmission in first gear.

*Answer: False, Page: 496, Difficulty Level - M

30.22 During a long extrication procedure, shock combined with temperature extremes can be fatal.

*Answer: True, Page: 498, Difficulty Level - M

30.23 An improvised or rigid cervical collar should be applied before alignment of the legs and body.

*Answer: True, Page: 498, Difficulty Level - M

30.24 Never waste time trying to gain access to a victim through the vehicle door. More likely than not, the door will be jammed.

*Answer: False, Page: 499, Difficulty Level - M

NOTES

NOTES

NOTES

NOTES

NOTES

NOTES

NOTES

NOTES